11+ COMPREHENSION PRACTICE PAPERS: VOLUME TWO

Model Answers & In-Depth Guided Explanations

R. P. DAVIS

Contents

Note on Volume Two   v
Foreword   vii

All Rounder Papers

Paper One: The Picture of Dorian Gray   3
Paper One: Model Answers & Guidance   11
Paper Two: The Secret Agent   23
Paper Two: Model Answers & Guidance   27

Close Language Papers

Paper Three: The Four Fists   39
Paper Three: Model Answers & Guidance   45
Paper Four: The Journey Out   55
Paper Four: Model Answers & Guidance   61

Line By Line Papers

Paper Five: Little Women   73
Paper Five: Model Answers & Guidance   77
Paper Six: Sister Carrie   87
Paper Six: Model Answers & Guidance   91

Speculative & Creative Papers

Paper Seven: Frankenstein   101
Paper Seven: Model Answers & Guidance   105
Paper Eight: Of Human Bondage   115
Paper Eight: Model Answers & Guidance   119

Endnotes   129

Note on Volume Two

Welcome to Accolade's second volume of 11+ comprehension papers.

The foreword that follows this note is largely unchanged from the foreword that appeared in the first volume, and contains all of the same "general" advice and guidance. Moreover, the way this book is structured is also much the same: eight papers, split into four subcategories (as explained in more depth in the foreword). However, each of the eight papers – plus the model answers – are wholly original. And while the analyses I offer for these model answers do repeat some of the guidance that appears in Volume 1, they are of course tailored to the new answers I have provided.

Foreword

When sitting 11+ comprehension exams at top schools (be they independent power-houses, or high-flying grammars) you will notice that, although all of their papers follow the basic formula – an extract accompanied by a set of questions – the *types* of questions they ask can vary greatly. The reason for this is simple enough: a considerable number of these schools write their papers in-house, and that means you find quirks in some papers that you don't in others. Even papers produced by examining bodies, such as the ISEB, have their idiosyncrasies. And yet, for all these quirks, there is still a *huge* degree of overlap between these various papers, because ultimately these schools are all looking for a similar set of skills.

As a result, preparing for these exams is eminently possible. We simply need to identify the various types of questions that appear (including those quirky ones!), then hone the skills required to answer them.

The intention of this guide is not simply to show you what these exams tend to look like (although, as you work through it, you will inevitably get a sense of this nonetheless!). No, the intention is to go a step further, and show you how to decode the sorts of questions these 11+ comprehension papers tend to ask, and what "perfect" answers to these questions look like. Moreover, it also seeks to explain, *in detail*, how exactly the model answers provided satisfy the examiners' criteria, making it as easy as possible for students to understand how to emulate these answers.

You will notice, also, that there are a number of questions for which I have supplied alternative answers. This is because, when it comes to comprehension papers, there are frequently instances where there is not *one* correct answer – instead, there are a number of potential answers that might be worthy of scoring the marks. The alternative answers are therefore included to demonstrate how there is, very often, room for flexibility and creativity.

Now, before I press on, I feel it is important to make one crucial thing clear: this guide is explicitly aimed at those students looking to achieve at the very highest level. Many times in this guide I use sophisticated vocabulary and ideas. I promise you that my intention is *not* to intimidate. Rather, we must remember that these are competitive exams, and that the grading is administered by human beings – so it is imperative that we dazzle these examiners, and give them no choice but to fork over the marks!

Rest assured, however, that when I use these tricky words or phrases, I explain them as I go. As a result, by the time you finish working through this guide, you should have a whole new arsenal of words and phrases to help you attack papers of any kind!

How This Book Is Set Out

As mentioned, 11+ papers are incredibly varied. However, if you spend enough time and energy looking through past papers, you start to figure out what makes them tick, and notice certain patterns that emerge time and again. This book contains eight papers that have been split into four different "styles" of questioning – two papers for each style. I have labelled the four types of papers as follows:

1) The All Rounder Paper

2) The Close Language Paper

3) The Line By Line Paper

4) The Speculative & Creative Paper

The labels I've given each style should give you some indication of what the papers entail. It may well be the case that some of the 11+ comprehension papers you end up taking fit neatly into the one of these styles. However, it is just as possible that they wind up being a blend of two (or more) styles – after all, schools often tweak the style of paper they put out year on year. At any rate, I can assert with confidence that, if you are well versed in all four styles, you will have your bases covered, and be prepared for most anything.

The questions for each paper appear twice. The first time they will appear is immediately after the extract, so that students can, if they wish, have a go at tackling the paper. They will then appear a second time, but this time accompanied by model answers and detailed guidance.

Each of the papers includes a "time guide" – that is, the amount of time one would expect to be given to complete the paper in an exam hall. If students wish to complete some of these papers as practice, I suspect this may prove useful.

Insofar as difficulty is concerned, the first paper in each style might be described as "hard," and the second "devilish." Again, I feel the need to reiterate that my intention is *not* to intimidate. On the contrary, by exposing students to the reality of what is in store, I believe it ensures that, when it actually comes to entering the exam hall, you feel far more at ease.

There is no *correct* way to use this guide. Some students will feel comfortable working through it by themselves, whereas some may prefer to have a parent at hand to act as a kind of surrogate tutor. In any case, the intention of this book is to give the reader the experience of having an experienced tutor at their beck and call.

Exam Tips

Within this book, you will find a good deal of question specific advice. However, there are a number of more general tips that it is important for any 11+ candidate to keep in mind:

- When reading the extract, don't rush. Some papers even set aside 10 minutes explicitly for reading the paper, and do not allow you to look at the questions until those 10 minutes have elapsed. This does not mean that 10 minutes is always necessary – but keep in mind that every school will expect you to read the passage very carefully.
- Read the questions carefully. It sounds obvious, I know, but you wouldn't believe how many times I have seen bright students lose marks simply because they have misread the question
- Always write in full sentences, unless you are explicitly told this is not required.
- If you are unhappy with an answer, and feel as though you must write something else, do not cross out your old answer until you have fully finished writing the new one – you may be throwing away precious marks!
- Keep quotes from the text short (unless explicitly told otherwise). As a rule of thumb, try and ensure that your quotes are no more than six or seven words in length, and preferably shorter.
- Most papers tell you how many marks a question is worth. Keep this in mind when working out how much time to spend on any given question.
- Remember: just because a question is, for instance, worth three marks, that does not necessarily mean you need to give three separate points. Of course there *are* occasions when three marks require three points, and I shall discuss those occasions in this book – but this is not *always* the case.
- Many 11+ papers give candidates blank lines on which to compose their

answers. When these appear, take them seriously: they are guidelines regarding how long the examiners would like your answer to be.

Personal Note

When I talk about my academic career, I usually talk about my time spent at university: I studied English Literature & Language at UCL, then took a Masters at Cambridge University. However, a mere twenty years ago, I was in the same position that many of my readers find themselves in: eager to win a place at a top secondary school, and faced with a litany of exams. Of course, the exams have changed a fair bit since then; but what I'm trying to say is, not only have I been teaching 11+ students for many years, but I've also had firsthand experience of it – I know what it's like to live through!

Even though I now look back on that time through a rosy lens – I was offered places at all the top London private and grammar schools I sat for – I won't pretend as though it was not at times intimidating. However, I would observe that many parts of the 11+ English exams, including many questions in the comprehension papers, offer rare opportunities not just to jump through hoops, but to exercise your powers of creativity. That is not to say that these exam are *fun* – my memory of them is pretty much the exact opposite – but still, it is important to at least try and embrace this creative element and enjoy the challenge.

All Rounder Papers

Note: This type of paper does not focus on one or two particular skills. Rather, the questions it asks tend to be varied, and require you to demonstrate a range of skills. You will find questions that require you to deduce information; questions that ask you to explain things in your own words; and questions that require mini-essays.

Both of the All Rounder papers I've included here are out of a total of fifty marks.

This passage is set in Victorian London. Dorian Gray has just murdered Basil Hallward, an artist who had painted a picture of Dorian Gray many years prior. The extract describes the events immediately following this murder.

1   He could hear nothing, but the drip, drip on the threadbare carpet. He opened the door and went out on the landing. The house was absolutely quiet. No one was about. For a few seconds he stood bending over the balustrade and peering down into the black seething well of darkness. Then he took out the key and returned to the
5   room, locking himself in as he did so.

The thing was still seated in the chair, straining over the table with bowed head, and humped back, and long fantastic arms. Had it not been for the red jagged tear in the neck and the clotted black pool that was slowly widening on the table, one would have said that the man was simply asleep.

10   How quickly it had all been done! He felt strangely calm, and walking over to the window, opened it and stepped out on the balcony. The wind had blown the fog away, and the sky was like a monstrous peacock's tail, starred with myriads of golden eyes. He looked down and saw the policeman going his rounds and flashing the long beam of his lantern on the doors of the silent houses. The crimson spot of a prowling
15   hansom gleamed at the corner and then vanished. A woman in a fluttering shawl was creeping slowly by the railings, staggering as she went. Now and then she stopped and peered back. Once, she began to sing in a hoarse voice. The policeman strolled over

and said something to her. She stumbled away, laughing. A bitter blast swept across the square. The gas-lamps flickered and became blue, and the leafless trees shook their black iron branches to and fro. He shivered and went back, closing the window behind him.

Having reached the door, he turned the key and opened it. He did not even glance at the murdered man. He felt that the secret of the whole thing was not to realize the situation. The friend who had painted the fatal portrait to which all his misery had been due had gone out of his life. That was enough.

Then he remembered the lamp. It was a rather curious one of Moorish workmanship, made of dull silver inlaid with arabesques of burnished steel, and studded with coarse turquoises. Perhaps it might be missed by his servant, and questions would be asked. He hesitated for a moment, then he turned back and took it from the table. He could not help seeing the dead thing. How still it was! How horribly white the long hands looked! It was like a dreadful wax image.

Having locked the door behind him, he crept quietly downstairs. The woodwork creaked and seemed to cry out as if in pain. He stopped several times and waited. No: everything was still. It was merely the sound of his own footsteps.

When he reached the library, he saw the bag and coat in the corner. They must be hidden away somewhere. He unlocked a secret press that was in the wainscoting, a press in which he kept his own curious disguises, and put them into it. He could easily burn them afterwards. Then he pulled out his watch. It was twenty minutes to two.

He sat down and began to think. Every year—every month, almost—men were strangled in England for what he had done. There had been a madness of murder in the air. Some red star had come too close to the earth.... And yet, what evidence was there against him? Basil Hallward had left the house at eleven. No one had seen him come in again. Most of the servants were at Selby Royal. His valet had gone to bed.... Paris! Yes. It was to Paris that Basil had gone, and by the midnight train, as he had intended. With his curious reserved habits, it would be months before any suspicions would be roused. Months! Everything could be destroyed long before then.

A sudden thought struck him. He put on his fur coat and hat and went out into the hall. There he paused, hearing the slow heavy tread of the policeman on the pavement outside and seeing the flash of the bull's-eye reflected in the window. He waited and held his breath.

After a few moments he drew back the latch and slipped out, shutting the door very gently behind him. Then he began ringing the bell. In about five minutes his valet appeared, half-dressed and looking very drowsy.

"I am sorry to have had to wake you up, Francis," he said, stepping in; "but I had forgotten my latch-key. What time is it?"

An extract from Oscar Wilde's The Picture of Dorian Gray

1) What time of day does the action in the passage take place? Be as specific as possible. [2]

....

....

2) Explain the meaning of the words that follow with regards to how they appear in the text. [12]

a) Seething (line 4)

....

b) Prowling (line 14)

....

c) Staggering (line 16)

....

d) Burnished (line 27)

....

e) Curious (line 37)

....

f) Roused (line 46)

....

3) Identify the simile used in the paragraph that starts: 'How quickly it had all been done!' [2]

....

....

....

4) Explain the effect of this simile. [2]

....

....

....

....

5) In your own words, explain why Dorian conceals the bag and coat he encounters in the library. [4]

....

....

....

....

....

....

....

....

6) The phrase "drip, drip, drip" is an example of what literary technique? [2]

....

....

7) Re-read lines 22 to 34 ('Having reached the door... his own footsteps'). Explain how the writer creates tension in this passage. Support your answer with evidence from these three paragraphs. [6]

8) The events in this extract take place in Dorian's London home. What is the name of Dorian's second home in the countryside? [3]

9) Look again at lines 39-53 ("He sat down to think... very drowsy"). How does the writer create a sense of danger in this portion of the story? [7]

....

....

....

....

....

....

....

....

....

....

....

....

10) What do you learn about the character of Dorian? Write in as much detail as you can and include evidence to support your point. [10]

....

....

1) What time of day does the action in the passage take place? Be as specific as possible. [2]

The action in the passage takes place in the early morning, for the most part just prior to 2 a.m.

Many 11+ papers like to start off with a quick 'warm up' question that requires you to play the part of a detective. On this occasion, it is all about attention to detail: the answer is lurking in the text, and it is simply a case of combing through and teasing it out.

At line 38, Dorian checks his watch, and notes that it is 'twenty minutes to two.' As a result, to score both marks here, you need to incorporate this detail into your answer. An answer that merely states the events took place in 'the early morning' or 'during the night,' without making reference to the specific time, would only garner one mark.

Note that, although brief, my answer above constitutes a full sentence. As a rule of thumb, *always* write in full sentences, unless you're explicitly told it is not necessary!

2) Explain the meaning of the words that follow with regards to how they appear in the text.

This style of question – that is, one that asks the candidate to give a definition of a word in light of its context – is a time-honoured favourite of 11+ examiners. In this paper, the candidate is presented with a list of words; however, other papers may ask for the definition of just one or two words.

Again, on this occasion, I am opting to use full sentences, since the exam paper has not given me permission to do otherwise.

When you are offering your definition, make sure you are using the same tense as the word you are defining. A good question to ask yourself is – would the word I'm using to define this fit seamlessly into the passage if I were to swap it in for the original word? If the answer is yes, you are on the right lines.

If you are uncertain of the meaning of any word, read the sentence within which it appears carefully – and, if need be, the sentences immediately preceding and proceeding it. In doing so, you might realise that you can make a decent educated guess. Remember, it is always better to make an educated guess than it is to leave the answer sheet blank.

a) Seething (line 4)

Seething here means simmering.

b) Prowling (line 14)

Prowling here means skulking or sneaking.

c) Staggering (line 16)

Staggering here means lurching.

d) Burnished (27)

Burnished here means polished.

e) Curious (37)

Curious here means idiosyncratic.

f) Roused (46)

Roused here means piqued.

3) Identify the simile used in the paragraph that starts: 'How quickly it had all been done!' [2]

The simile is as follows: '…the sky was like a monstrous peacock's tail.'

Remember, similes are comparisons that make use of either the word 'as' or 'like.' On this occasion, the writer uses the word 'like' to formulate a simile.

Notice that I am not quoting the entire sentence. Rather, I'm quoting just the relevant snippet that contains the simile. The ellipsis (three dots) before the quote indicates that it appears mid-sentence.

4) Explain the effect of this simile. [2]

By likening the sky to a peacock's tail, the writer on one level seems to imply that it is a sight of extravagant and remarkable beauty, since peacocks' plumage is known for its outlandish beauty; indeed, the implication is that the sky is also seductive, for male peacocks display their tails to attract sexual partners. However, by comparing the sky not just to a peacock's tail, but, paradoxically, to a monstrous one (one does not expect something beautiful to be monstrous), the writer hints there is something sinister or excessive about the sky's aesthetic beauty, thereby subtly reminding the reader of the sinister goings-on within Dorian's house. [1]

There are a number of ways of approaching this question: after all, the simile works on a number of levels. Above, I have discussed three separate effects the simile achieves: namely, that it draws attention to the sky's remarkable beauty; that it suggests the sky might be construed as sexually seductive; and that its monstrousness echoes the monstrousness of the murder. In all likelihood, any two of those points would have been enough to secure the two marks that are up for grabs. However, I personally encourage students to go that extra mile – to include that extra observation – since we don't want to give the examiner any opportunity to dock marks.

It might be added, also, that the points I've made in my answer are not the only points you could have made. You might, for instance, have discussed how a peacock's tail takes the shape of a semicircle, and thus this simile could arguably have been drawing attention not just to the sky's aesthetics, but also its shape as it appeared to Dorian. Alternatively, given that peacock's tails are constantly expanding and contracting, one could have instead inferred that the simile was suggesting that the night's sky appeared to be in flux.[2] Any of these approaches would have likely scored you marks.

As an aside, as you might have noticed, I am not holding back with my vocabulary. Please don't be intimidated by this. The fact of the matter is: the very top schools are looking for the best and the brightest – so building your vocabulary can only be a good thing. For the record, something's aesthetics are basically how they look. You will also notice that I've inserted a footnote in the answer. Footnotes such as this appear throughout the guide, and you can use them to look up explanations for words and phrases I've used.

5) In your own words, explain why Dorian conceals the bag and coat he encounters in the library. [4]

Dorian conceals the bag and coat he encounters in the library because they clash with the story he intends to feed the authorities. Dorian indicates that Basil (the man he has murdered) had already left his house once already a few hours earlier, and had had plans to catch a train to Paris. Dorian indicates, also, that he believes that nobody would have seen Basil re-enter his premises. As a result, he intends to tell the authorities that Basil had left his home and had not returned, while also disposing of all the evidence that contradicts this narrative: Basil's body; his bag and coat. However, since he does not currently have the time to destroy Basil's personal effects, Dorian has hidden them temporarily.

Questions that ask you to put things 'in your own words' are another perennial favourite of 11+ question writers. The basic premise is that, if you are able to explain an element of the passage in your own words, you demonstrate that you truly understand it.

As the phraseology of the question implies, it's important to try as best you can to avoid the vocabulary used in the extract – you can see that my explanation, beyond the words 'bag' and 'coat,' has been written with entirely fresh vocabulary.

Although there are four marks in play, when it comes to 'in your own words' questions, this does not necessarily mean you need to write four different things. Clarity is king; so I'm scoring those four marks chiefly through the accuracy and coherency of my answer. It is imperative that your answer acknowledges that Dorian is hiding the bag and coat to conceal the fact that Basil had returned to his home, and he does this with the ultimate aim of covering up his crime from the authorities. Indeed, if you fail to acknowledge this ultimate objective, you answer will likely be capped at two marks.

6) The phrase "drip, drip, drip" is an example of what literary technique? [2]

The above phrase is an example of onomatopoeia.[3]

We do not require two points in order to score both marks here. We simply need to have the right answer.

Unfortunately, for a question like this, you simply need to know the answer. My advice: make sure you brush up on literary techniques and technical terms in general. You will encounter more within this guide, which should help build up your knowledge base.

7) Re-read lines 22 to 34 ('Having reached the door... his own footsteps'). Explain how the writer creates tension in this passage. Support your answer with evidence from these three paragraphs. [6]

A key mechanism the writer uses to create tension is the staging: Dorian seems to find it incredibly difficult to extricate himself from the scene of the crime.[4] **His first attempt to leave the room sees him 'reach[ing] the door' and 'turn[ing] the key and open[ing]...in' – the writer seemingly including these details to slow the action to an excruciating snail's pace – only to then find himself drawn back in by the sudden imperative to deal with the lamp. Yet if this thwarted attempt to leave the room leaves the reader tense, the successful departure that ensues shortly after does little to dispel this tension, since the personified woodwork, which 'seemed to cry out as if in pain' as Dorian descends the stairs, ensures the motif of violence follows Dorian even as he puts distance between himself and his crime.**

Tension is also generated through the vivid description of Basil's corpse itself. The short staccato sentences, made all the more abrupt by the doubling up of exclamation marks – 'How still it was! How horribly white...!' – induce in the reader a breathlessness that mirrors Dorian's own, vicariously involving the reader in this close-up with the cadaver.[5] **Moreover, while the story may be written in the third person, the use of free indirect style here, which frames events firmly from Dorian's point of view, also creates a tense immediacy for the reader, tacitly implicating them in the crime this body attests to.**[6] **That the corpse is likened to a**

'dreadful wax image' suggests a tense, unnerving proximity that allows Dorian to register the very texture of its skin.

The sense that Dorian's own mind is conspiring against him further contributes to the tension in this passage. Dorian notes that to fend off the psychological trauma, the 'secret' is to 'not realize the situation.' However, mere moments later, Dorian is drawn back into the room and up-close to the corpse, thereby forcing him to 'realize' the situation – the implication being that his mind's defences have been compromised. This is evidenced in the next paragraph. The way Dorian stops 'several times and waited,' only to then conclude that 'everything was still' and 'it was merely the sound of his own footsteps,' suggests he had momentarily convinced himself he was not alone in the house, his paranoia further stoking tension.[7]

Right, there's plenty to say about the question and answer above.

First off, we're told that it's worth six marks; but since almost every top private school marks these papers internally, and publish no standardised mark schemes, it's impossible to know whether they want you to make two points or three.

I personally advocate a "cover all your bases" mentality: if you can think of three points, and you can back them all up, then you make it very tough for the examiner to withhold marks. That said, if you can only identify two points in the heat of the exam, but can argue them well, you may still find yourself scoring over four marks.

Another key thing to keep in mind when answering a question of this kind – that is, a question that asks you to focus on a 'mini' passage within the extract – is to make sure you do not just focus on one part of this mini passage. You need to take the whole of the mini passage into account.

Now, let's look at the actual substance of my answer.

The first thing I ought to mention on this front is the fact that I did not simply dive into writing. Rather, I took a couple of minutes beforehand to construct a short, sharp plan. This is something I always do when dealing with questions that require more meaty answers – because this allows me to know exactly where I'm taking my argument, and it leads to greater focus and precision. My plan looked like this:

- The seeming difficulty in leaving the room: the room draws him back in; the stairs creak accusatively as he exits.
- The description of the body.
- Dorian's own mind turning on itself.

Crucially, the question asked me to *explain* – and it also gave me broad scope to use any kind of evidence I deemed appropriate. As a result, I ensured that my answer did not just look closely at the language used, but also at factors such as pacing and narrative techniques. In doing so, I demonstrated to the examiner an understanding that the writer uses a range of tools to realise his aims.

You'll also notice that I talk at one point about the 'free indirect third person.' I know this sounds like an intimidatingly technical phrase, but let me explain.

You may already know that a first person story is one written from a character's own point of view ('I went there. I did this'), and that a third person story is one in which a narrator describes the actions of the story's character's ('He did this. She did that'). But have you ever noticed how, when you are reading a third person story, it sometimes still feels as if you are subtly getting a certain character's distinct point of view? As if the narrator perhaps has a secret insight into that character's mind? Well, this is known as the 'free indirect third person;' and, while technically still a type of third person narration, it feels a bit like a blend between first person and third person.

Examiners like it when you have sophisticated technical vocabulary up your sleeve. I want you to be able to spot it when you see it, as I have done here.

Finally, I'd observe that questions relating to tension – e.g. *how does the writer create tension, or how does the writer make the passage tense*, and so forth – are fairly popular, so do make sure you feel ready to tackle questions of this kind.

<u>8) The events in this extract take place in Dorian's London home. What is the name of Dorian's second home in the countryside?</u>

Dorian's second home is called Selby Royal.

This question – like the first one in this paper – once again requires you to play the sleuth. Yet this particular question is a little trickier, because while Selby Royal is mentioned at line 43 as the location where Dorian's servants are currently residing, it is never explicitly spelt out that this is Dorian's countryside home. However, the fact we are being asked this question in the first place tells us the answer *must* be lurking in the extract somewhere; and it is reasonable to deduce – in the absence of any explicit clue that would indicate otherwise – that Dorian's servants would be assembled at his second home.

<u>9) Look again at lines 39-53 ("He sat down to think... very drowsy"). How does the writer create a sense of danger in this portion of the story? [7]</u>

The write conjures a palpable sense of the danger Dorian finds himself in by having Dorian meditate on the punishment that lays in wait should he be caught. Dorian reflects how 'Every year – every month, almost – men were strangled,' a reference to the public hangings of convicted murderers. Not only does this crystallize the precarious position Dorian finds himself in, but the sentence itself, comprising as it does of an interpolated phrase clamped between two dashes, ensures the form reflects this threat of asphyxiation.[8] The image of a 'red star…too close to the earth' enhances this sense of abstract danger, evoking a scenario in which the earth's inhabitants (Dorian included) are at risk from some kind of interstellar cataclysm.[9]

If contemplations on the law represent a kind of abstract, theoretical danger, this passage also conveys the more immediate sense of the danger Dorian faces. Chiefly responsible for this is the police officer who, with his 'slow heavy tread,' happens to be moving past Dorian's front door as he prepares to instigate his cover-up. The long sentence combined with the evident physical proximity of the officer – Dorian can see his 'bull's-eye reflected in the window' – forces the reader to fully grapple with the presence of this ambassador of the law, who has the power to scupper Dorian's plans and enforce the dire fate he had been mulling. That Dorian is induced to wait and 'h[o]ld his breath' indicates Dorian's own appreciation for the danger – he is deeply anxious not to alert the policeman to his presence – and vicariously invites the reader to feel the danger just as keenly.

The writer does work not only to convey a sense of the danger Dorian faces, but also the danger he represents to others. After contemplating the punishments he faces, Dorian not only reminds us of his own capacity for murder – 'a madness of murder in the air' – but gear-shifts to contemplating his cover-up with frightening clarity: how he intends to take advantage of the fact 'No one had seen [Basil] come in again' to contend that Basil had taken 'the midnight train' to Paris, and to destroy all evidence ('everything'). As a result, as Dorian comes into proximity to others – the officer, his valet – the writer creates a sense not only of the danger Dorian faces, but also that he represents to others.

Given the time constraints, it seems unlikely that the examiners are looking for four separate points to score the seven marks here. So, instead, I decided to put together an answer comprising of three points, and simply made sure to delve into each of them in plenty of detail.

Notice how, once again, I break things down into distinct ideas. Before I started writing, I wrote three quick bullet points:

- The abstract danger Dorian faces.
- The more concrete danger represented by the police officer.
- The danger Dorian represents to others.

It is, if you like, a very brief essay plan, and it ensured that I knew where I was going when I started writing.

You will notice also that my final argument subtly plays on expectations: whereas the examiner will likely expect answers to focus on the dangers Dorian faces, I have chosen to focus also on the danger he represents to others. Before attempting a slightly more adventurous approach of this kind, the key is to read the question carefully, because while you want to impress the examiner, you must also be sure that your response is still answering the question. In this instance, the question was asking about 'a sense of danger' in general, and did not limit us to just the dangers Dorian faces.

10) What do you learn about the character of Dorian? Write in as much detail as you can and include evidence to support your point. [10]

Dorian is in many respects portrayed as a fastidiously cunning individual.[10] This is evidenced by the way that Dorian, shortly after committing murder, quickly takes steps to cover his tracks – for example, he removes the lamp, since its location could alert 'his servant' to unusual goings-on, and places Basil's 'bag and coat' in a 'secret press' in the 'wainscoting.' Indeed, that this 'secret press' even exists, and is full of 'curious disguises,' hints at a history of underhand and cunning behaviour: the sort of behaviour that would have required phoney identities. Yet Dorian's cunning is not only embodied in what he does, but what he plans to do. Dorian considers in detail the narrative he hopes to spin – that Basil has gone to 'Paris' – and how to make it convincing: by destroying Basil's possessions.

Galvanising this fastidiously cunning behaviour appears to be another character trait in Dorian: a strain of paranoia.[11] After all, implicit in his decision to move the lamp is the fear that his servant may act against him. However, while this is a clear indication of his paranoia, the trait is also hinted at more subtly throughout the passage: for instance, the way Dorian peers over the 'balustrade' into the 'seething well of darkness' indicates an anxiety that intruders may be near, and so too does the way he 'stopped several times and waited' on the stairs.

However, although Dorian may exhibit paranoia, he also exhibits a profound confidence in his own abilities to convincingly dissemble.[12] This is perhaps best exemplified by the bold move to beckon Francis at the end of the extract, and to enact his plan to make it seem as though he has just arrived home ('I had forgotten my latch-key'). We do not discover how Francis reacts to this performance; yet the very fact Dorian dares to carry it out so soon after committing murder points to a confidence that borders on hubris.[13]

Another key aspect of Dorian's character is his deep attunement to detail. This is perhaps best exemplified when he briefly steps onto the balcony, and pays particular attention to minutiae: he picks up on, among other things, 'the doors of the silent houses,' the 'crimson spot' of the 'hansom,' a woman's 'fluttering shawl,' and the 'black iron branches' of the 'leafless trees.'[14] However, not only is Dorian profoundly observant, but he also seems greatly interested in the aesthetic qualities of his environment. This is particularly striking when Dorian focuses his gaze on the 'lamp.' Despite being in the middle of a high-stakes cover-up, he spends a surprising amount of time parsing the lamp's aesthetic qualities: its 'Moorish workmanship,' the 'burnished steel,' the studding 'with coarse turquoises.'[15] Dorian's eye is not only sharp, but it is drawn to stimuli of particular aesthetic interest.[16]

Questions of this kind – that is, *"what do you learn about the character of X?"* questions – are seen in comprehension papers from a number of top schools, though they sometimes appear with slightly different phrasing: for instance, *"what are your impressions of Character X?"*

The key thing here is not to simply start writing, but to take a moment to draw out a few distinct observations regarding the character in question. On this occasion, since 10 marks were in play, I made sure to use four points, since three would likely have been too few. I'm counting on the fact that each point will win me, at a minimum, two marks, and that a couple of my points are sophisticated enough, and written with sufficient flair, that the examiner will feel inclined to award them three points.

As with the previous question, I also made a mini plan before I started writing, which took the form of four brief bullet points:

- Fastidiously cunning.
- Paranoid.
- Confident in capacity to deceive.

- Attuned to details in his environs.

Because I had these four "themes," I knew exactly what I wanted to write. This tactic ensures you have direction and clarity as you set about writing.

You'll notice also that I always back my points up with quotes from the text. These quotes are rarely long – usually no more than about six or seven words – and they are almost always integrated into the flow of sentence. This is what you ought to be striving for! Simply dumping very long quotes into your work is unlikely to impress: they want to see that you have the ability to extract the most relevant material.

I also want to add that the arguments I've made above are not exhaustive – you might have made another argument that is just as valid as those I've pursued, and that will still have won you marks. For example, we might have written a paragraph about Dorian's utter lack of moral compass – in fact, to demonstrate, I shall insert a paragraph on this theme below, written in the style of 'alternative' final paragraph to the one I opted for in the end:

That Dorian feels so comfortable dissembling points to another apparent trait in him: his total absence of a moral compass. It is striking that in the wake of committing murder, Dorian exhibits no compunction.[17] On the contrary: he seems pleased that he had dispatched the individual who had induced in Dorian 'misery' through his 'fatal portrait.' Indeed, that he calls his victim a 'friend' while observing the advantageousness of his death further draws attention not only to his monstrous lack of ethics, but also his utter lack of empathy: Dorian's so-called friend's right to life is less important than his own comfort.

This novel is set in London in the early twentieth century. Mr Verloc is preparing to go to bed as the household winds down for the night.

---

1   He took the cash-box out of the drawer, and turning to leave the shop, became aware
     that Stevie was still downstairs.

     What on earth is he doing there? Mr Verloc asked himself. What's the meaning of
     these antics? He looked dubiously at his brother-in-law, but he did not ask him for
5   information. Mr Verloc's intercourse with Stevie was limited to the casual mutter of
     a morning, after breakfast, "My boots," and even that was more a communication at
     large of a need than a direct order or request. Mr Verloc perceived with some
     surprise that he did not know really what to say to Stevie. He stood still in the middle
     of the parlour, and looked into the kitchen in silence. Nor yet did he know what
10   would happen if he did say anything. And this appeared very queer to Mr Verloc in
     view of the fact, borne upon him suddenly, that he had to provide for this fellow too.
     He had never given a moment's thought till then to that aspect of Stevie's existence.

     Positively he did not know how to speak to the lad. He watched him gesticulating
     and murmuring in the kitchen. Stevie prowled round the table like an excited animal
15   in a cage.

     A tentative "Hadn't you better go to bed now?" produced no effect whatever; and Mr
     Verloc, abandoning the stony contemplation of his brother-in-law's behaviour,

crossed the parlour wearily, cash-box in hand. The cause of the general lassitude he felt while climbing the stairs being purely mental, he became alarmed by its inexplic-

20 able character. He hoped he was not sickening for anything. He stopped on the dark landing to examine his sensations. But a slight and continuous sound of snoring pervading the obscurity interfered with their clearness. The sound came from his mother-in-law's room. Another one to provide for, he thought—and on this thought walked into the bedroom.

25 Mrs Verloc had fallen asleep with the lamp (no gas was laid upstairs) turned up full on the table by the side of the bed. The light thrown down by the shade fell dazzlingly on the white pillow sunk by the weight of her head reposing with closed eyes and dark hair done up in several plaits for the night. She woke up with the sound of her name in her ears, and saw her husband standing over her.

30 "Winnie! Winnie!"

At first she did not stir, lying very quiet and looking at the cash-box in Mr Verloc's hand. But when she understood that her brother was "capering all over the place downstairs" she swung out in one sudden movement on to the edge of the bed. Her bare feet, as if poked through the bottom of an unadorned, sleeved calico sack

35 buttoned tightly at neck and wrists, felt over the rug for the slippers while she looked upward into her husband's face.

"I don't know how to manage him," Mr Verloc explained peevishly. "Won't do to leave him downstairs alone with the lights."

She said nothing, glided across the room swiftly, and the door closed upon her white

40 form.

Mr Verloc deposited the cash-box on the night table, and began the operation of undressing by flinging his overcoat on to a distant chair. His coat and waistcoat followed. He walked about the room in his stockinged feet, and his burly figure, with the hands worrying nervously at his throat, passed and repassed across the long strip

45 of looking-glass in the door of his wife's wardrobe. Then after slipping his braces off his shoulders he pulled up violently the venetian blind, and leaned his forehead against the cold window-pane—a fragile film of glass stretched between him and the enormity of cold, black, wet, muddy, inhospitable accumulation of bricks, slates, and stones, things in themselves unlovely and unfriendly to man.

50 Mr Verloc felt the latent unfriendliness of all out of doors with a force approaching to positive bodily anguish. There is no occupation that fails a man more completely than that of a secret agent of police. It's like your horse suddenly falling dead under you in the midst of an uninhabited and thirsty plain. The comparison occurred to Mr Verloc because he had sat astride various army horses in his time, and had now

55 the sensation of an incipient fall.   The prospect was as black as the window-pane against which he was leaning his forehead.

An extract from Joseph Conrad's The Secret Agent

1) What colour garment do you think Mrs Verloc is wearing? [2]

2) Explain the meaning of the words that follow with regards to how they appear in the text. [12]

    a) Dubiously (line 4)

    b) Gesticulating (line 13)

    c) Lassitude (line 18)

    d) Inexplicable (lines 20-21)

    e) Dazzlingly (line 26)

    f) Inhospitable (line 48)

3) Identify the simile that appears in the paragraph that begins: 'Positively he did not know how...' [2]

4) Explain the effect of this simile. [2]

5) In your own words, explain why Mr Verloc decides to wake Mrs Verloc. [4]

6) '"What on earth is he doing there?" Mr Verloc asked himself.' The quote above is an example of what literary technique? [2]

7) Re-read lines 16 to 30 ('A tentative... "Winnie! Winnie"). Explain how the writer creates tension in this passage. Support your answer with evidence from these three paragraphs. [6]

8) What do you think Mr Verloc's job might be? Justify your answer. [3]

9) Look again at lines 37-56 ("I don't know how... leaning his forehead"). How does the writer create a sense of doom in this portion of the story? [7]

10) What do you learn about the character of Mr Verloc? Write in as much detail as you can and include evidence to support your point. [10]

```
┌─────────────────────────────────────┐
│                                     │
│      Paper Two: Model Answers &     │
│              Guidance               │
│                                     │
└─────────────────────────────────────┘
```

<u>1) What colour garment do you think Mrs Verloc is wearing?</u> [2]

I think Mrs Verloc's garment is white.

Again, this type of question is ensuring that you are paying attention to details, though it is slightly tougher than the opening question in the previous paper, as it requires a bit more inference. At lines 39-40, we are told that the 'door closed upon [Mrs Verloc's] white form.' This is the best clue we are given, and from it we can deduce that Mrs Verloc's garment is likely white.

We are also told that she is wearing a 'calico sack;' however, calico is a type of fabric, *not* a colour.

<u>2) Explain the meaning of the words that follow with regards to how they appear in the text.</u> [12]

a) Dubiously (line 4)

Dubiously here means uncertainly.

b) Gesticulating (line 13)

Gesticulating here means waving [his] limbs expressively.

c) Lassitude (line 18)

Lassitude here means weariness.

d) Inexplicable (lines 20-21)

Inexplicable here means unexplainable.

e) Dazzlingly (line 26)

Dazzlingly here means incandescently.

f) Inhospitable (line 48)

Inhospitable here means unwelcoming.

3) Identify the simile that appears in the paragraph that begins: 'Positively he did not know how...' [2]

The simile is as follows: 'Stevie prowled round the table like an excited animal in a cage.'

Once again we have a simile that makes use of the word 'like.' On this occasion, because the simile appears in a short sentence, I have quoted the sentence in its entirety.

4) Explain the effect of this simile. [2]

By likening Stevie and his movements to an excited animal in a cage, the writer not only gives a sense of the manner in which he is moving – just as a caged animal moves back and forth across a small surface area, so too is Stevie – but also invites the reader to project onto Stevie traits one would associate with a caged wild animal – unpredictability, dangerousness, frustration – since wild animals are the type most likely to be caged in the first place. Moreover, the imagery of the cage invites us to conceive of Verloc's home as an oppressive, prison-like domain; a place that causes Stevie to feel boxed-in and trapped.

Again, as I did for the fourth question in the previous paper, I have articulated three different ways in which this simile works: it deepens our understanding of how Steve moves; it invites us to project onto him the traits one would associate with a wild animal; and it casts Verloc's home as a kind of prison. It is likely that any two of these points would have been enough to score the two marks up for grabs; yet, as ever, I'm playing it safe and slotting in a third point.

5) In your own words, explain why Mr Verloc decides to wake Mrs Verloc. [4]

> **The reason Mr Verloc wakes his wife is to do with Stevie. Mr Verloc wishes to wind down the household for the night. However, whereas Mr Verloc does not wish to leave anyone downstairs as he prepares to head upstairs to bed himself, not only is Stevie still in the downstairs parlour, but he is also unresponsive when Mr Verloc attempts to coax him upstairs. As a result of this, Mr Verloc – feeling incapable of eliciting the reaction from Stevie he is looking for – wakes Mrs Verloc in the hopes that she will be better equipped to convince Stevie to turn in.**

Remember, when it comes to questions of this kind, your chief objective is clarity. You need to get across the fact that Mr Verloc wants to get Stevie to turn in for the night, that he feels as if he is unable to do so, and that, as a result, he turns to Mrs Verloc for help. Each of those observations are worth one mark apiece, whereas the fourth is for the coherency and sophistication of your answer – have you explained these points in a flowing and eloquent way that can truly be described as your own words?

6) '"What on earth is he doing there?" Mr Verloc asked himself.' The quote above is an example of what literary technique? [2]

> **This quote is an example of inner monologue.**

This question does *not* require two separate points: they simply want you to demonstrate that you understand the literary technique in question, and that you are aware of the technical phrase that is used to describe it.

7) Re-read lines 16 to 30 ('A tentative... "Winnie! Winnie"). Explain how the writer creates tension in this passage. Support your answer with evidence from these three paragraphs. [6]

The use of Gothic imagery is a particularly potent mechanism by which the writer generates tension in this passage.[1] While perhaps simple, the darkness that cloaks Verloc as he hits the top of the stairs – 'the dark landing' – effectively creates an air of unease and tension, and the intrusion of the 'slight and continuous sound of snoring,' a bizarre and idiosyncratic soundtrack, only heightens the unease.[2] Perhaps most significant, however, is the presence of Stevie as a Gothic outsider, a status earned in no small part through his detachment from human interaction: Verloc's attempt to engage him 'produce[s] no effect whatever.'[3] Stevie's sheer otherness thus adds yet another Gothic element to the mix, further ramping up the tension.

Also effective in stoking tension is the sense of responsibility that seems to oppress Verloc. As Verloc comes within earshot of his mother-in-law's snoring, he reflects how she represents 'another one to provide for' – the word 'another' reminding us how Verloc had previously meditated on the need to provide for Stevie. Moreover, immediately after this reflection, Verloc encounters Mrs Verloc 'asleep,' and this structural progression implicitly invites us to entertain the possibility that Mrs Verloc may be another dependent. By going to such lengths to explore the anxieties Verloc feels over his responsibility, the writer tacitly introduced the tense possibility that Verloc may suddenly soon become unable to provide.

That Verloc appears to be in ailing mental and physical health is yet another source of tension in this passage. Not only does Verloc register a weariness ('lassitude') in himself as he mounts the stairs, but he also understands it to be the product of his 'mental' state. Moreover, in expressing hope he is not 'sickening,' Verloc simply further draws attention to the fact he may very well be doing just that; and the way he lingers on these sensations – 'he stopped...to examine these sensations' – forces the reader to extend their meditation on their unnerving import, too. Indeed, by using a free indirect third person style that conveys events from Verloc's point of view, the author ensures the reader vicariously shares in this anxiety-ridden deterioration, thus redoubling the sense of tension.

Six marks are up for grabs in this question. To play it safe, I decided to make three distinct points, ensuring that each point I included was detailed enough to secure at least two marks apiece.

As I have mentioned before, when presented with a question of this kind, I would *not* suggest starting to write immediately. Instead, have a think about what you'd like to say, and put together an incredibly quick plan, so you can write with coherency and direction. I picked out three "themes" before starting, and wrote the following (very brief) bullet points for myself as prompts:

- The use of Gothic tropes, such as darkness and setting; Stevie as an outsider.
- Verloc's overwhelming sense of responsibility for others.
- Verloc's sense of mounting illness.

At all times, the fact I've been asked to *explain* is at the front and centre of my mind, and I am continually making clear how the theme I've identified – be it the gothic setting, or Verloc's ailing state – is used to create tension. This is vital: it ensures that you are always answering the question!

8) What do you think Mr Verloc's job might be? Justify your answer. [3]

One might deduce that Mr Verloc is a 'secret agent of police,' since he meditates on the difficulties of that line of work in tandem with reflecting on his own sense of foreboding.[4] Moreover, while Mr Verloc does seem to run a 'shop' and is tending to a 'cash-box' at the start of the extract, this could still be consistent with being a secret agent, for the shop may be a cover for his true occupation.

This is a fairly devilish question, because the start of the passage is misleading: after all, one might see the references to the 'money box' and the 'shop' in the first sentence and be forgiven for jumping to the conclusion that Verloc runs a shop. However, near the end of the extract, Mr Verloc explores his sense of foreboding in practically the same breath as his dim meditations on the occupation of 'the secret agent of police,' and this very powerfully implies that *this* is in fact his occupation. With this in mind, one realises that running a shop is not his job; it is something he does because secret agents need to be discreet, so the shop is his 'cover' – something to distract people's attention from his true profession.

One mark is for the correct answer. The two further marks are for justifying the answer coherently.

9) Look again at lines 37-56 ("I don't know how... leaning his forehead"). How does the writer create a sense of doom in this portion of the story? [7]

One might note that the aloofness and detachment of those with whom Verloc attempts to interact is a key ingredient for infusing this passage with doom.[5] In response to Verloc's comment that it 'won't do to leave [Stevie] downstairs,' Verloc receives no reply from Mrs Verloc. On the contrary, the writer explicitly spells out that 'she said nothing' prior to exiting the room. If this aloofness isolates Verloc, thus creating a sense of doom, Verloc's comment that 'I don't know how to manage him' reminds the reader that Stevie, too, refuses to verbally engage Verloc, thus redoubling the sense of isolation and doom.

Not only do Verloc's co-inhabitants induce a sense of doom with their inhospitability, but so too does the cityscape that he encounters as he 'lean[s] his forehead against the cold window-pane.' The writer piles up adjectives that capture the hostile environment the city embodies – it is 'cold, black, wet, muddy' – but also dissects the city itself into disparate fragmented parts – 'bricks, slates, and stones' – thereby suggesting that the city offers nothing substantial on which Verloc might visually or emotionally latch onto to allay his sense of doom.[6] His conclusion that his environment is 'unlovely and unfriendly to man' is not only in itself a conclusion steeped in foreboding, but also an uncannily apt description of how Stevie and Mrs Verloc treat Verloc: they seem both 'unlovely and unfriendly.'

Mr Verloc's body language also contributes to the sense of impending doom. Indeed, his manner seems to be exactly what one would expect from an individual suffering from fraught nerves: his 'hands' are 'worrying at his throat' (the verb 'worrying,' usually very much abstract, given a physical literalism); he is pacing back and forth ('passed and repassed'); and he finds himself slumped against the window.[7] Yet though Verloc's body language conveys his sense of doom, his inner monologue, disclosed via the free indirect narrative, does so even more effectively. Verloc uses a simile to liken his professional situation to being aboard 'a horse' that suddenly falls 'dead...in the midst of an uninhabited plain,' implying that he has been left in a dire situation. Moreover, Verloc has the 'sensation of an incipient fall' – a sentiment that explicitly evokes doom – and, to hammer the point home, likens the sensation to the blackness of the 'window-pane.'

Again we have a question that asks us to focus on a passage within the extract. Again, although the word 'explain' is not explicitly used, the 'how does...' formulation indicates that we are indeed required to offer an explanation. Again, the seven marks in the context of a 'mini essay' type question points towards the need for at least three substantial points – each point earning at least two points, and an extra point to be earned through sophistication of ideas, quality of argument, and so forth.

True to form, before I started writing, I put together one of my very brief plans:

- The aloofness and detachment of those with whom Verloc lives.
- The doom created by the cityscape beyond his window.
- Verloc's body language & inner monologue.

10) What do you learn about the character of Mr Verloc? Write in as much detail as you can and include evidence to support your point. [10]

A key plank of Verloc's personality appears to be his sense of responsibility. Near the start of the extract, Verloc, as he watches Stevie, is found reflecting on how 'he had to provide for this fellow,' and this motif recurs when Verloc hears his mother-in-law snoring and muses that she is 'another one to provide for.' However, while Verloc comes across as responsibility-minded, one might also note that it appears to be a newfound trait: indeed, though Stevie has presumably long been a dependent, the notion of Stevie's dependency is 'borne upon [Verloc] suddenly,' as if it had not occurred to Verloc hitherto.

Verloc's interactions with Stevie also reveal another facet to Verloc: that he is brusque and undemonstrative in nature.[8] This is exemplified not only in how Verloc addresses Stevie in a bid to coax him to bed – 'Hadn't you better go to bed now?' – but also in his historical interactions with Stevie. Indeed, it is revealed that generally the only words Verloc addresses to Stevie are 'My boots:' two monosyllabic, brusque words that keep the interaction to a minimum.[9] Verloc's brusqueness is on display again as he wakes Winnie up: the exclamation 'Winnie! Winnie!' is a markedly abrupt way of rousing someone from their sleep. Moreover, whereas one might expect a husband to wake a wife with some affection, and perhaps even make use of physical contact, this particular interaction is utterly undemonstrative on Verloc's part.

Verloc comes across as a cripplingly uncertain individual. Verloc multiple times, for example, expresses uncertainty with how to deal with Stevie: the reader is told that Verloc 'did not really know what to say to Stevie;' that he 'did not know how to speak to the lad,' and he directly tells Mrs Verloc that he does not 'know how to manage' Stevie. His

uncertainty is so extreme that, prior to addressing Stevie, Verloc also exhibits uncertainty with regards to how Stevie might react: 'He did not know what would happen.' Yet Verloc's uncertainty goes beyond Stevie; for instance, the writer tells us that Verloc 'hoped he was not sickening.' Implicit in this comment is an uncertainty concerning his own state: even despite stopping to 'examine his sensations,' Verloc is ultimately unsure whether he is in fact 'sickening.'

Verloc is also characterised by a tendency to watch and observe others. As Stevie prowls the kitchen 'like an excited animal,' the writer explicitly notes how Verloc 'watched,' thereby drawing attention to Verloc's role as observer. Verloc also seems to observe the tableau of the sleeping Mrs Verloc in meticulous detail, noting the 'lamp...turned up,' the 'light thrown down by the shade,' the 'pillow sunk by the weight of her head.'[10] The focus on minutiae once again casts Verloc as a voyeur; as someone who watches.[11] This tendency to watch is levelled not only at people, but the city, too, which he scans through 'the cold window-pane.'

The passage also reveals something of Verloc as a physical entity. As he undresses, the reader is informed that he is a 'burly' figure, and the way he physically interacts with his environment – in particular, the way he 'fling[s] his overcoat on to a distant chair' and 'pulled up violently the venetian blind' – hints that he is unsubtle and somewhat raw with his motions. While it may be tricky to extrapolate anything concrete about his personality from these details, they nevertheless further expand our understanding of Verloc as a character.

On this occasion, my plan contained five relevant points:

- Takes his responsibilities seriously.
- Brusque and undemonstrative.
- Profoundly uncertain.
- A proclivity for watching others.[12]
- Physically burly; rough with how he interacts with his environment.

However, I knew, insofar as timing was concerned, that it was unrealistic to try and tackle all five in depth. As a result, I decided that I would tackle three in great depth, and two (the fourth and fifth point) briefly. Even if the shorter points were to garner, say, three marks between them, I'd still feel comfortable with the prospect of scoring seven marks from my three more meaty points.

As it so happens, a sixth theme also occurred to me during the planning stage: the fact that Verloc appears to be a deeply nihilistic individual.[13] Although I decided not to include this argument in the end (if only because my answer was already long enough already), it once again illustrates that – when it comes to meaty questions of this kind – there are often multiple lines of argument that can plausibly win you marks.

Close Language Papers

Note: While the next two papers do share some similarities with the first two – again, we have short questions asking us to deduce things, spot details, and define certain words – the higher-scoring questions in this paper are inviting us to look closely at the writer's choice of language and to discuss these choices in explicit detail. In many respects, this style of paper is more focused: you do not need to write mini essays in quite the same way – rather, the name of the game is demonstrating your intimate understanding of individual quotations. Indeed, the questions themselves are often more detailed, frequently making it explicit what they wish to see from you.

Both of the Close Language papers I've included here are out of a total of forty marks.

This extract, set in the early twentieth century, explores the experience of Samuel Meredith as he starts at a boarding school.

1   It all started at Phillips Andover Academy when he was fourteen. He had been brought up on a diet of caviar and bell-boys' legs in half the capitals of Europe, and it was pure luck that his mother had nervous prostration and had to delegate his education to less tender, less biassed hands.

5   At Andover he was given a roommate named Gilly Hood. Gilly was thirteen, under-sized, and rather the school pet. From the September day when Mr. Meredith's valet stowed Samuel's clothing in the best bureau and asked, on departing, "hif there was hanything helse, Master Samuel?" Gilly cried out that the faculty had played him false. He felt like an irate frog in whose bowl has been put goldfish.

10   "Good gosh!" he complained to his sympathetic contemporaries, "he's a damn stuck-up Willie. He said, 'Are the crowd here gentlemen?' and I said, 'No, they're boys,' and he said age didn't matter, and I said, 'Who said it did?' Let him get fresh with me, the ole pieface!"

For three weeks Gilly endured in silence young Samuel's comments on the clothes
15   and habits of Gilly's personal friends, endured French phrases in conversation, endured a hundred half-feminine meannesses that show what a nervous mother can do to a boy, if she keeps close enough to him—then a storm broke in the aquarium.

Samuel was out. A crowd had gathered to hear Gilly be wrathful about his room-mate's latest sins.

20 "He said, 'Oh, I don't like the windows open at night,' he said, 'except only a little bit,'" complained Gilly.

"Don't let him boss you."

"Boss me? You bet he won't. I open those windows, I guess, but the darn fool won't take turns shuttin' 'em in the morning."

25 "Make him, Gilly, why don't you?"

"I'm going to." Gilly nodded his head in fierce agreement. "Don't you worry. He needn't think I'm any ole butler."

"Le's see you make him."

At this point the darn fool entered in person and included the crowd in one of his
30 irritating smiles. Two boys said, "'Lo, Mer'dith"; the others gave him a chilly glance and went on talking to Gilly. But Samuel seemed unsatisfied.

"Would you mind not sitting on my bed?" he suggested politely to two of Gilly's particulars who were perched very much at ease.

"Huh?"

35 "My bed. Can't you understand English?"

This was adding insult to injury. There were several comments on the bed's sanitary condition and the evidence within it of animal life.

"S'matter with your old bed?" demanded Gilly truculently.

"The bed's all right, but——"

40 Gilly interrupted this sentence by rising and walking up to Samuel. He paused several inches away and eyed him fiercely.

"You an' your crazy ole bed," he began. "You an' your crazy——"

"Go to it, Gilly," murmured some one.

"Show the darn fool——"

45 Samuel returned the gaze coolly.

"Well," he said finally, "it's my bed——"

He got no further, for Gilly hauled off and hit him succinctly in the nose.

"Yea! Gilly!"

"Show the big bully!"

50   "Just let him touch you—he'll see!"

The group closed in on them and for the first time in his life Samuel realized the insuperable inconvenience of being passionately detested. He gazed around helplessly at the glowering, violently hostile faces. He towered a head taller than his roommate, so if he hit back he'd be called a bully and have half a dozen more fights on his hands

55   within five minutes; yet if he didn't he was a coward. For a moment he stood there facing Gilly's blazing eyes, and then, with a sudden choking sound, he forced his way through the ring and rushed from the room.

The month following bracketed the thirty most miserable days of his life. Every waking moment he was under the lashing tongues of his contemporaries; his habits

60   and mannerisms became butts for intolerable witticisms and, of course, the sensitiveness of adolescence was a further thorn. He considered that he was a natural pariah; that the unpopularity at school would follow him through life.

An extract from F. Scott Fitzgerald's The Four Fists

1. The following is a comprehension question. As such, only short answers are required.

a) In which continent did Samuel spend his childhood? [1]

b) The passage states that Samuel grew up on a diet of 'bell-boys' legs.' What does this suggest about his living situation prior to school? [1]

c) In which month of the year does Samuel start at Philips Andover Academy? [1]

d) Why do you think Samuel's valet's speech contains spelling mistakes? ('hif there was hanything helse') [1]

e) What do you think Gilly is trying to convey when he claims the 'faculty had played him false'? Is it that:

- The faculty had misrepresented his new roommate's personality beforehand.
- The faculty, by lodging him with Samuel, had betrayed him.
- The faculty had not told Gilly a valet would be accompanying Samuel.

Circle the answer that appears most correct. [1]

2. This question tests your ability to discuss language. The following three quotations are taken from between lines 9 and 30. Explain how the writer conveys a sense of tension and ill will between Gilly and Samuel. Your ability to discuss the meanings of individual words and to identify literary techniques (such as metaphors or similes) will be rewarded.

   a) 'He felt like an irate frog in whose bowl has been put goldfish.' [3]

   b) '...then a storm broke in the aquarium.' [3]

   c) 'At this point the darn fool entered in person and included the crowd in one of his irritating smiles.' [2]

   d) Look back at lines 1 – 31. What is your overall impression of Gilly? Using adjectives (describing words) and any quotation NOT used in the exam so far, write your answer below. [3 marks; 12 marks total for this question].

3. This question tests your understanding of character. Think about the character of Samuel. In your own words, explain what the following two quotations say about his character:

   a) There were several comments on the bed's sanitary condition and the evidence within it of animal life. [3]

   b) The group closed in on them and for the first time in his life Samuel realized the insuperable inconvenience of being passionately detested. [3]

4. This question tests your ability to explain the meanings of words as they appear in the passage. Work out the meaning of the following words based on their meaning in the passage. [6]

   a) Biassed (line 4)

   b) Meannesses (line 16)

   c) Perched (line 33)

   d) Succinctly (line 47)

   e) Glowering (line 53)

   f) Lashing (line 59)

5. This question tests your ability to find a quotation and explain its meaning.

a) Find a quote that explicitly explores the impact Samuel's mother has had on his life, and explain what kind of impact it suggests Samuel's mother has had on him.

QUOTATION [1]

EXPLANATION [3]

6. This question tests your ability to explain the meanings of quotations. In your own words, and based on the context of the passage, explain why the writer has written the following:

a) "Just let him touch you—he'll see!"' [2]

b) '...so if he hit back he'd be called a bully and have half a dozen more fights on his hands within five minutes; yet if he didn't he was a coward.' [3]

c) He considered that he was a natural pariah; that the unpopularity at school would follow him through life. [3]

1. The following is a comprehension question. As such, only short answers are required.

a) In which continent did Samuel spend his childhood? [1]

In Europe.

To score the mark here, you really do need the specific answer I've given above. Notice how I did not use a complete sentence. This is because the question has explicitly told us that only 'short answers are required.'

b) The passage states that Samuel grew up on a diet of 'bell-boys' legs.' What does this suggest about his living situation prior to school? [1]

It suggests he was living at hotels, since that is where bell-boys work.

The key inference here is that Samuel had been living at hotels, and getting this right very much hinges on the candidate having heard the expression bell-boy. A bell-boy traditionally greets guests and takes their bags up to their room at a hotel.

c) In which month of the year does Samuel start at Philips Andover Academy? [1]

Samuel commenced study in September.

Again, to score the mark here, you must have the correct answer – September – and there is no inference involved. It is simply a case of combing the text carefully and spotting the right detail (which is at line 6).

d) Why do you think Samuel's valet's speech contains spelling mistakes? ('hif there was hanything helse') [1]

The speech contains spelling mistakes in order to convey the fact the valet has an accent.

The key thing to acknowledge here is that spelling mistakes have been used to convey the valet's accent – the word 'dialect' would likely also score the mark. However, if a candidate says something along the lines of "it is used to show the valet speaks differently," they are unlikely to gain the mark.

e) What do you think Gilly is trying to convey when he claims the 'faculty had played him false'? Is it that:

- The faculty had misrepresented his new roommate's personality beforehand.
- **The faculty, by lodging him with Samuel, had betrayed him.**
- The faculty had not told Gilly a valet would be accompanying Samuel.

Circle the answer that appears most correct. [1]

You occasionally see a one-off multiple choice question in papers that are otherwise *not* multiple choice papers.

When such questions appear, there is often at least one option that seems plausible, yet is in fact incorrect – it's what we might call the 'stumbling block' option. To 'play someone false' can mean to betray someone, but it can also mean to mislead someone (in fact, if you think about it, there are scenarios in which these meanings could be linked – after all, it is possible to betray someone by misleading them). However, there is no indication whatsoever in this particular situation that the faculty had misrepresented Samuel's personality to Gilly beforehand. As a result, the second option – that

Gilly is expressing his belief that the faculty has betrayed him – is the most likely meaning of Gilly's comment.

2. This question tests your ability to discuss language. The following three quotations are taken from between lines 9 and 30. Explain how the writer conveys a sense of tension and ill-will between Gilly and Samuel. Your ability to discuss the meanings of individual words and to identify literary techniques (such as metaphors or similes) will be rewarded.

a) 'He felt like an irate frog in whose bowl has been put goldfish.' [3]

> **The writer, by making use of a simile that likens Gilly to 'an irate frog' and Samuel to a 'goldfish,' suggests that tension is inevitable, since it is implying that placing these boys together is akin to placing into close proximity two greatly different species, one of whom has a predisposition towards being 'irate', and considers the territory its own ('whose bowl').[1] Indeed, by likening the room to a 'bowl,' the writer creates a sense of their cohabitation being on show for all to see, thereby upping the tension, as it places a greater onus on not losing face for both parties.[2]**

Correctly identifying the simile the author uses is almost certainly good to win you a mark; and the two extra observations I've included – that it emphasises the fact that the two boys are very different, and that their conflict has been made into a public spectacle – are likely to be worth an extra mark apiece.

b) '...then a storm broke in the aquarium.' [3]

> **The writer, with the notion that 'a storm broke in the aquarium,' is in fact layering a metaphor on top of the simile he has already invoked – the one suggesting the boys in the room are akin to a frog and goldfish in a bowl. The idea of a metaphorical 'storm' breaking out suggests that the tension between the two parties has given way to outright displays of ill-will – displays that possess something of the tumult of a storm. However, the idea of a 'storm' in an 'aquarium' is also reminiscent of the idiom of a storm in a teacup, implying that, while there is undoubtedly ill-will and tumult between the boys, the point of contention has been blown out of proportion.**

This is a tricky question, because the phrase you are being asked to analyse cannot be disentangled from the simile used in 'part a' of this question. As a result, merely discussing how the writer employs the metaphor of a 'storm' to convey drama and acrimony won't get you more than one mark; rather, to get all three marks, the candidate must also acknowledge that the phrase under analysis is making use of the simile that had previously likened the boys to animals.

There is one caveat to the above. You will notice that in the last sentence of my answer, I introduce a new point: that the writer's phraseology appears to play on the idiom 'a storm in a teacup.' At this point, I had already scored three marks, and thus my extra argument was for good measure. However, if a student rightly observes that the quote under analysis makes use of the metaphor of a storm, yet fails to link it back to the previous simile (which, as mentioned, would limit them to one mark), they could still earn a second mark by identifying the play on the idiom.

c) 'At this point the darn fool entered in person and included the crowd in one of his irritating smiles.' [2]

> **That the writer has the narrator here refer to Samuel as 'the darn fool'**
> **indicates that the narrator is expressing things from Gilly's point of view**
> **– indeed, the phraseology exactly echoes Gilly's earlier description of**
> **Samuel – and reiterates Gilly's sense of disdain and antipathy towards**
> **Samuel.**[3] **Not only does describing Samuel's smile as 'irritating' further**
> **underscore the ill-will Samuel induces in Gilly, but there is great irony in**
> **the use of the word 'included,' since the grating nature of his smile in**
> **fact ends up excluding him from the group and alienating Samuel further**
> **from Gilly.**

The reason the exam paper has offered up two marks for analysing this quote, yet three marks for the previous two quotes, is because this quote is arguably less challenging, since it does not contain any similes or metaphors.

To score two marks here, you need to be sure not just to focus in on one part of the sentence. Above, I have analysed three phrases within the sentence: 'the darn fool,' 'included the crowd,' and 'irritating smile.' Truth be told, if you had analysed any two of these phrases effectively, you would likely score both marks.

d) Look back at lines 1 – 31. What is your overall impression of Gilly? Using adjectives (describing words) and any quotation NOT used in the exam so far, write your answer below. [3 marks; 12 marks total for this question].

A fitting adjective to describe Gilly might be indulged. One of the first things the reader learns about Gilly is that he was 'rather the school pet,' the phrase 'pet' suggesting that he had been coddled by staff and students alike.[4] That the other boys who crowd about him prior to the physical altercation vocally support Gilly and take umbrage on his behalf – 'Don't let him boss you'; 'Show the darn fool' – further creates a sense that Gilly is indulged by those around him.[5]

Another apt adjective to describe him might be pugnacious. The writer all but describes him as such when he notes that Gilly speaks 'truculently;' in other words, that he takes a tone as if spoiling for a fight. Yet the best evidence of Gilly's pugnacity is of course the fact that, in the face of fairly slight provocation – Samuel is merely complaining about the fact his bed is being sat on by Gilly's buddies – Gilly resorts to physical violence: he 'hit [Samuel] succinctly in the nose.'

Another suitable adjective to describe Gilly might be proud. Interestingly, it appears that Gilly, in private, has put up with behaviour he disliked from Samuel without resorting to violence: he complains, for instance, that Samuel 'won't take turns shuttin' [the windows] in the morning.' It is only when Samuel crosses him while others are watching, and indeed egging him on ('Show the big bully!'), that Gilly feels the need to shield his pride and save face with violence.[6]

There are resonances in this question to the one in the previous style of paper that asked us what we learned about a character within the extract. However, the difference here is that we need to be far more selective, and far more succinct – after all, this is a three mark question, so we can infer that they likely require three adjectives, each accompanied by a brief explanation.

Even though we need to be brief, it is important to try and capture the complexity of the character in question. For instance, though Gilly is indulged by those around him, and one might expect this dynamic to take pressure off him in everyday life, that same indulgence in fact puts him at the centre of attention, thereby creating a scenario in which he is under pressure to save face (and, in turn, reveal his deep-seated pride). The tension between the adjectives I've chosen indicates my sensitivity to nuance.

3. This question tests your understanding of character. Think about the character of Samuel. In your own words, explain what the following two quotations say about his character:

a) There were several comments on the bed's sanitary condition and the evidence within it of animal life. [3]

Samuel here is levelling insults at Gilly's friends, but is doing so in a subtle, oblique way: instead of explicitly calling Gilly's friends sitting on his bed filthy animals, Samuel slyly suggests his bed is dirty and infested.[7] By making the insult cryptic, Samuel demonstrates that he is less interested in simple name-calling, and more interested in punishing the other children with his intelligence; after all, it would seem his intention it to have the other children initially fail to understand his insult, and to feel stupid for not being able to discern its meaning.[8] That he makes multiple comments of this kind perhaps suggests an arrogance: he feels as if, with his insults suitably cloaked, he can get away with running his mouth as much as he pleases.

In a sense, this style of question (much like the one just before it) is still asking you to demonstrate a close understanding of the language used. However, this time you are not required to analyse the language techniques. Instead, by making using of the 'in your own words' formula, the examiner is asking you to demonstrate understanding by offering an explanation.

Acknowledging that Samuel is insulting the other children – he is referring to them as unsanitary animals – is worth one mark, and a second mark is at stake for understanding that he is intentionally veiling his insults, so that they go over the other children's heads, thereby making them feel stupid.[9] A third mark is for acknowledging the sense of self-assuredness, or even arrogance, this winking style of insult reveals in Samuel.

b) The group closed in on them and for the first time in his life Samuel realized the insuperable inconvenience of being passionately detested. [3]

That Samuel has reached adolescence and never felt the sensation of being hated suggests that he has had a sheltered existence that has ensured that he had never before come face-to-face with such antipathy. However, Samuel does not appear to take the situation as an indictment of him personally or experience any kind of hit to his self-esteem; rather, he appears to construe it as a frustrating circumstance that must somehow be overcome and resolved. This points to Samuel's pragmatic worldview, but also perhaps an inner sense of self worth.[10]

The first mark is for understanding how this quote reveals the sheltered life Samuel has led up until this point; the second is for registering that his reaction to the hatred – a reaction not of reciprocated animus, but of a sense of inconvenience – demonstrates his pragmatic worldview.[11] The third mark is for the clarity and coherency of your answer.

4. This question tests your ability to explain the meanings of words as they appear in the passage. Work out the meaning of the following words based on their meaning in the passage. [6]

a) Biassed (line 4)

Biassed here means blinkered.

b) Meannesses (line 16)

Meannesses here means cruelties.

c) Perched (line 33)

Perched here means squatted.

d) Succinctly (line 47)

Succinctly here means unhesitatingly.

e) Glowering (line 53)

Glowering here means scowling.

f) Lashing (line 59)

Lashing here means punishing.

5. This question tests your ability to find a quotation and explain its meaning.

a) Find a quote that explicitly explores the impact Samuel's mother has had on his life, and explain what kind of impact it suggests Samuel's mother has had on him.

QUOTATION [1]

"...Gilly...endured a hundred half-feminine meannesses that show what a nervous mother can do to a boy, if she keeps close enough to him."

EXPLANATION [3]

> **The phrase 'half-feminine meannesses' refers to passive-aggressive insults and behaviours: this is due to sexist societal biases that associate displays of aggression with masculinity, and passive-aggression with femininity. The implication here is that Samuel's mother not only made these kinds of comments in Samuel's company, but exposed him to such comments and behaviour to an enormous degree; after all, the writer is suggesting that she kept him overly close ('if she keeps close enough to him'). The result of this, the writer suggests, is that Samuel's mother had rubbed off on him, and Samuel has thus taken to using the same style of insult.**

The quote I have picked above is the one you need to score the first mark. You may notice that I used an ellipsis (three dots) not only before the quote, but in the middle of the quote, too: this indicates to the reader that you are leaving out words that are not required to make your point, and this can save time. Do be careful when using this tactic, though: you still need to convey the meaning of the quote coherently.

The difficulty on the analytical front is deciphering the phrase 'half-feminine meannesses' – two marks are at stake for understanding that the phrase refers to passive-aggressive behaviour, and that passive aggression (as opposed to outright aggression) was historically associated with women due to societal stereotypes. A third mark is for recognising that the writer suggests this behaviour was instilled in Samuel as a result of his closeness to his mother.

6. This question tests your ability to explain the meanings of quotations. In your own words, and based on the context of the passage, explain why the writer has written the following:

a) "Just let him touch you—he'll see!'" [2]

> **The writer has included this snippet of speech – an exclamation from one of the other boys crowded into Gilly and Samuel's room – to convey the peer pressure Gilly is under to physically confront Samuel and save face, but also, given the comment's acrimonious tone and the exclamation mark, to create a general sense of tumult and heightened emotions.[12] That the comment is not attributed to any boy in particular adds to the sense of tumult and confusion, while also subtly implying that the words speak for all in attendance, and that this hostility is felt by the crowd as a whole.**

The phrasing of this question is a bit tricky: it is not simply asking why the character (one of the other schoolboys) says the above; it is asking why the writer has put those words in the schoolboy's mouth. When answering a question about why the writer chose to do something, it is sensible to write in such a way that acknowledges this distinction between the writer and the character.

The first mark is for observing how the writer uses this comment to convey the peer pressure Gilly is under. The second is for understanding how the comment – its lack of specific provenance in particular – adds to a sense of general confusion and tumult.[13]

b) '...so if he hit back he'd be called a bully and have half a dozen more fights on his hands within five minutes; yet if he didn't he was a coward.' [3]

The writer's aim here is to dissect the paradox Samuel faces with this opportunity to retaliate: he is in between a metaphorical rock and a hard place, since any course of action will have negative consequences. On the one hand, retaliating will invoke the wrath of Gilly's contemporaries; on the other, he risks looking craven should he back down.[14] The writer includes this to further emphasise Samuel's pragmatic mindset: even in this tense situation, Samuel still has a clear sense of the risks involved with both courses of action. Finally, by pointing out how pacifism is equated with cowardice in this all-male environment, the author deftly captures the way in which gender expectations haunt the minds of schoolboys.[15]

Two marks are reserved for not just acknowledging that the writer uses this to explore the paradox Samuel finds himself in, but also for explaining the nature of this paradox: the fact that he is 'damned if he does, damned if he does not.'[16] The third mark is for adding another sensible observation – for instance, the fact that the writer uses the quote to convey Samuel's pragmatism; or the fact it conveys how this all-male environment equates pacifism with weakness.

c) He considered that he was a natural pariah; that the unpopularity at school would follow him through life. [3]

The chief purpose of this sentence is to allow the writer to communicate Samuel's mindset and feelings in the aftermath of this altercation – namely, his sense that he was born to be an outcast.[17] That he feels that

this ostracisation will persist throughout his life is the writer's way of communicating the fact that Samuel, for all his pragmatism, still has a child-like way of looking at the world: he naively feels as though his fate in perpetuity is set in stone.[18] Samuel's overblown, even histrionic tone may also be the writer's way of subtly signalling to the reader that in fact the opposite is true; that Samuel's future will in fact see him enjoy the acceptance he craves.[19]

One mark is available for discussing how the writer uses this to explore Samuel's sense of ostracisation after the fight. Another mark can be gained for acknowledging how the exaggerated emotions Samuel experiences are used to remind the reader of his youth and naivety. A third mark can be gained for understanding that the quote in fact hints that the opposite will be true – that Samuel will find himself very much accepted by his contemporaries.

This novel is set in the early twentieth century and follows the lives of English people holidaying in South America. This particular extract describes Helen Ambrose's experiences at a tea party.

1   The first thing that caught Helen's eye as she came downstairs was a carriage at the door, filled with skirts and feathers nodding on the tops of hats. She had only time to gain the drawing-room before two names were oddly mispronounced by the Spanish maid, and Mrs. Thornbury came in slightly in advance of Mrs. Wilfrid Flushing.

5   "Mrs. Wilfrid Flushing," said Mrs. Thornbury, with a wave of her hand. "A friend of our common friend Mrs. Raymond Parry."

Mrs. Flushing shook hands energetically. She was a woman of forty perhaps, very well set up and erect, splendidly robust, though not as tall as the upright carriage of her body made her appear.

10   She looked Helen straight in the face and said, "You have a charmin' house."

She had a strongly marked face, her eyes looked straight at you, and though naturally she was imperious in her manner she was nervous at the same time. Mrs. Thornbury acted as interpreter, making things smooth all round by a series of charming commonplace remarks.

15   "I've taken it upon myself, Mr. Ambrose," she said, "to promise that you will be so kind as to give Mrs. Flushing the benefit of your experience. I'm sure no one here

knows the country as well as you do. No one takes such wonderful long walks. No one, I'm sure, has your encyclopaedic knowledge upon every subject. Mr. Wilfrid Flushing is a collector. He has discovered really beautiful things already. I had no

20 notion that the peasants were so artistic—though of course in the past—"

"Not old things—new things," interrupted Mrs. Flushing curtly. "That is, if he takes my advice."

The Ambroses had not lived for many years in London without knowing something of a good many people, by name at least, and Helen remembered hearing of the

25 Flushings. Mr. Flushing was a man who kept an old furniture shop; he had always said he would not marry because most women have red cheeks, and would not take a house because most houses have narrow staircases, and would not eat meat because most animals bleed when they are killed; and then he had married an eccentric aristocratic lady, who certainly was not pale, who looked as if she ate

30 meat, who had forced him to do all the things he most disliked—and this then was the lady. Helen looked at her with interest. They had moved out into the garden, where the tea was laid under a tree, and Mrs. Flushing was helping herself to cherry jam. She had a peculiar jerking movement of the body when she spoke, which caused the canary-coloured plume on her hat to jerk too. Her small but

35 finely-cut and vigorous features, together with the deep red of lips and cheeks, pointed to many generations of well-trained and well-nourished ancestors behind her.

"Nothin' that's more than twenty years old interests me," she continued. "Mouldy old pictures, dirty old books, they stick 'em in museums when they're only fit for burnin'."

40 "I quite agree," Helen laughed. "But my husband spends his life in digging up manu- scripts which nobody wants." She was amused by Ridley's expression of startled disapproval.

"There's a clever man in London called John who paints ever so much better than the old masters," Mrs. Flushing continued. "His pictures excite me—nothin' that's old

45 excites me."

"But even his pictures will become old," Mrs. Thornbury intervened.

"Then I'll have 'em burnt, or I'll put it in my will," said Mrs. Flushing.

"And Mrs. Flushing lived in one of the most beautiful old houses in England—Chill- ingley," Mrs. Thornbury explained to the rest of them.

50 "If I'd my way I'd burn that to-morrow," Mrs. Flushing laughed. She had a laugh like the cry of a jay, at once startling and joyless.

"What does any sane person want with those great big houses?" she demanded. "If you go downstairs after dark you're covered with black beetles, and the electric lights

55 always goin' out. What would you do if spiders came out of the tap when you turned on the hot water?" she demanded, fixing her eye on Helen.

Mrs. Ambrose shrugged her shoulders with a smile.

"This is what I like," said Mrs. Flushing. She jerked her head at the Villa. "A little house in a garden. I had one once in Ireland. One could lie in bed in the mornin' and pick roses outside the window with one's toes."

60 "And the gardeners, weren't they surprised?" Mrs. Thornbury enquired.

"There were no gardeners," Mrs. Flushing chuckled. "Nobody but me and an old woman without any teeth. You know the poor in Ireland lose their teeth after they're twenty. But you wouldn't expect a politician to understand that—Arthur Balfour wouldn't understand that."

65 Ridley sighed that he never expected any one to understand anything, least of all politicians.

An extract from Virginia Woolf's The Journey Out

---

1. The following is a comprehension question. As such, only short answers are required.

   a) Whose names do you think the Spanish maid speaks out loud? [1]

   b) In which room does Mrs Ambrose meet Mrs Flushing? [1]

   c) Who does Mrs Thornberry identify as Mrs Flushing's and Mrs Ambrose's mutual friend? [1]

   d) At whose home does the tea party take place? [1]

   e) Mrs Ambrose sees a carriage 'filled with skirts and feathers nodding on the tops of hats.' What do you think can be inferred from this? Is it that:

   • The carriage is filled with spare clothes and hats for the guests.
   • The carriage contains people wearing skirts and hats.
   • The carriage contains exotic birds for the guests to admire.

   Circle the answer that appears most correct. [1]

2. This question tests your ability to discuss language. The following three quotations are taken from between lines 11 and 51. Explain how the writer conveys a sense of

Mrs Flushing's personality and appearance. Your ability to discuss the meanings of individual words and to identify literary techniques (such as metaphors or similes) will be rewarded.

a) 'She had a strongly marked face, her eyes looked straight at you, and though naturally she was imperious in her manner she was nervous at the same time.' [2]

b) 'Her small but finely-cut and vigorous features, together with the deep red of lips and cheeks, pointed to many generations of well-trained and well-nourished ancestors behind her.' [3]

c) 'She had a laugh like the cry of a jay, at once startling and joyless.' [3]

d) Look back at lines 1 – 51. What is your overall impression of Mrs Flushing? Using adjectives (describing words) and any quotation NOT used in the exam so far, write your answer below. [3 marks; 12 marks total for this question].

3. This question tests your understanding of character. Think about the character of Mrs Thornbury. In your own words, explain what the following two quotations say about her character.

a) Mrs. Thornbury acted as interpreter, making things smooth all round by a series of charming commonplace remarks. [3]

b) "'I've taken it upon myself, Mr. Ambrose," she said, "to promise that you will be so kind as to give Mrs. Flushing the benefit of your experience.'" [3]

4. This question tests your ability to explain the meanings of words as they appear in the passage. Work out the meaning of the following words based on their meaning in the passage. [6]

a) Splendidly (line 8)

b) Carriage (line 8)

c) Encyclopaedic (line 18)

d) Eccentric (line 29)

e) Disapproval (line 42)

f) Intervened (line 46)

5. This question tests your ability to find a quotation and explain its meaning.

a) Mrs Ambrose's husband, Ridley, is present throughout the passage. Using a quotation to back up your view, what do you think his job might be?

QUOTATION [1]

EXPLANATION [3]

6. This question tests your ability to explain the meanings of quotations. In your own words, and based on the context of the passage, explain why the writer has written the following:

a) "What would you do if spiders came out of the tap when you turned on the hot water?" [3]

b) 'Mrs. Ambrose shrugged her shoulders with a smile.' [2]

c) 'Ridley sighed that he never expected any one to understand anything, least of all politicians.' [3]

Paper Four: Model Answers & Guidance

1. The following is a comprehension question. As such, only short answers are required.

a) Whose names do you think the Spanish maid speaks out loud? [1]

The maid calls out the names Mrs. Wilfrid and Mrs. Flushing

It was a tradition at parties to have a member of staff announce the arrival of a guest to the room. Even if a student did not know this, they still might have been able to deduce the answer based on the fact that Mrs. Wilfrid and Mrs. Flushing are the individuals mentioned directly after the reader is told that the maid 'mispronounced' two names.

In any case, the mark will only be awarded if the candidate mentions *both* names.

b) In which room does Mrs. Ambrose meet Mrs. Flushing? [1]

Mrs. Ambrose meets Mrs. Flushing in the drawing-room.

This question simply requires the student to be paying attention to detail. The fact they meet in the drawing-room is mentioned at line 3.

c) Who does Mrs. Thornberry identify as Mrs. Flushing's and Mrs. Ambrose's mutual friend? [1]

Mrs. Raymond Parry is identified as their mutual friend.

Again, this question requires a keen eye for detail, but little in the way of deduction. The answer can be found at line 6.

d) At whose home does the tea party take place? [1]

At Mrs. Ambrose's home.

At line 10, Mrs. Flushing says to Mrs. Ambrose: 'You have a charmin' house.' Given that Mrs. Flushing has just arrived at the house, we can infer that the house at which this party is taking place is Mrs. Ambrose's.

e) Mrs. Ambrose sees a carriage 'filled with skirts and feathers nodding on the tops of hats.' What do you think can be inferred from this? Is it that:

- The carriage is filled with spare clothes and hats for the guests.
- **The carriage contains people wearing skirts and hats.**
- The carriage contains exotic birds for the guests to admire.

Circle the answer that appears most correct. [1]

Whereas in the previous paper there were two options that were fairly similar, all three options here are quite stark. Although 'feathers' are mentioned, the fact that 'skirts' and 'hats' are also mentioned should alert us to the fact that we are *not* dealing with exotic birds, which eliminates the third option. Moreover, that the feathers are 'nodding on the tops of hats' implies that people are wearing these hats (the motion of their heads are causing the feathers to move back and forth). As a result, the idea that these are simply 'spare clothes and hats' (*option a*) can also be eliminated.

2. This question tests your ability to discuss language. The following three quotations are taken from between lines 11 and 51. Explain how the writer conveys a sense of Mrs Flushing's personality and appearance. Your ability to discuss the meanings of

individual words and to identify literary techniques (such as metaphors or similes) will be rewarded.

a) 'She had a strongly marked face, her eyes looked straight at you, and though naturally she was imperious in her manner she was nervous at the same time.' [2]

> **The above quotation captures a tension in how Mrs. Flushing presents herself: whereas to be 'imperious' would usually connote self-assurance and self-possession – it is a word one might associate with a ruler or a monarch, and that she is 'naturally' so hints at an authenticity – she is oxymoronically also identified as 'nervous,' which undercuts the gravitas.[1] Moreover, while Mrs Flushing's eyes chiefly serve to enhance the sense of imperiousness as opposed to nervousness, since unwavering eye-contact ('she looked straight at you') is usually associated with unwavering nerves, her 'strongly marked face' is more enigmatic: it suggests her face bears the imprint of experience, yet it does not elaborate on what those experiences might entail.[2]**

'Part a' of this question is worth two marks (as opposed to the three marks parts b and c are both worth) because there are no similes or metaphors for us to identify.

There are various observations that have the potential to score you one of the two marks. Observing the tension between her nervousness and her imperious manner (which I've described as oxymoronic) is worth a mark. You would also gain a mark for discussing the significance of her eye contact (it lends her an intensity, and perhaps even a gravitas). A sensible analysis of her 'strongly marked face' – perhaps commenting on the strength it imbues her, or her age or experience – would also be worthy of a mark.

b) 'Her small but finely-cut and vigorous features, together with the deep red of lips and cheeks, pointed to many generations of well-trained and well-nourished ancestors behind her.' [3]

> **The chief conceit here – that Mrs. Flushing's 'vigorous features' and 'deep red... lips and cheeks' reveal the levels of wealth ('well-nourished') and education ('well-trained') her ancestors enjoyed – invites the reader to not simply take these aesthetic details at face value, but to see them as indicators of Mrs. Flushing's aristocratic pedigree; to perhaps even read the word 'vigorous' as a euphemism for haughty, and to deduce that Mrs Flushing's appearance and manner likely indicate that she too is 'well-**

trained' and 'well-nourished'.[3] **This subtext aside, these physical descriptors are interesting in their own right, too. For instance, by describing her features as 'finely-cut,' the wrier uses a metaphor to convey Mrs Flushing's precise, statuesque face.**

This is a significantly more difficult quote to analyse.

One mark is reserved for correctly identifying that 'finely-cut...features' represents a metaphor. This metaphor is very subtle – it would be more obvious if her features were described, for instance, as 'statuesque.' Nevertheless, her features are not *literally* finely-cut, and identifying this correctly as a metaphor is necessary.

The other two marks are for demonstrating an understanding that Mrs Flushing's other physical features are used by the writer as a means to communicate something of Mrs Flushing's aristocratic and educated background. If a candidate makes other strong comments about Mrs Flushing's appearance or background, but does not observe how the writer creates a link between the two, they can only be awarded one of the other two marks up for grabs.

c) 'She had a laugh like the cry of a jay, at once startling and joyless.' [3]

The central simile here likens Mrs. Flushing's 'laugh' to the 'cry of a jay,' suggesting that both a jay's cry and Mrs. Flushing's laugh are 'startling and joyless.' That her laugh is 'startling' hints at a performativeness that suggests that Mrs Flushing uses it to sate a craving for attention, whereas the idea it is 'joyless' hints at an inner unhappiness; after all, while laughter is usually shorthand for joy, Mrs Flushing's laugh ironically embodies the exact opposite.[4] **Likening the laugh to that of a small bird in general gives Mrs. Flushing's manner an air of absurdity, and insinuates that the personality behind it is as lacking in sophistication as a 'jay.'**

One mark here is reserved for correctly identifying that the writer makes use of a simile that likens Mrs. Flushing's laugh to the cry of a jay.

To gain the other two marks, you need to make two further substantial observations: for instance, you could discuss the effect the writer achieves by paradoxically describing Mrs. Flushing's laugh as joyless; or the fact the sentence hints that Mrs. Flushing has bird-like traits in a wider sense; or perhaps the 'startling' quality of Mrs. Flushing's laugh and what it suggests about her personality. Any one of these would be worth a mark; though, as stated, you would be capped at two if you fail to identify the simile.

d) Look back at lines 1 – 51. What is your overall impression of Mrs. Flushing? Using adjectives (describing words) and any quotation NOT used in the exam so far, write your answer below. [3 marks; 12 marks total for this question].

> **A particularly fitting adjective to describe Mrs. Flushing might be disruptive. This trait is perhaps best exemplified in the impact she had on her husband's life. Mrs. Ambrose reflects that Mr. Flushing, prior to meeting Mrs. Flushing, was a man deeply set in his ways: he was someone who 'always said he would not marry' and 'would not take a house' and 'would not eat meat,' and the list goes on. However, after entering his life, Mrs Flushing utterly disrupted Mr Flushing's strict mantras, and 'forced him to do all the things he most disliked.'**
>
> **Mrs Flushing also comes across as irreverent.[5] This characteristic is best illustrated in her opinions on cultural artefacts, and her conviction that, instead of belonging in museums, 'old pictures' and 'old books' are 'only fit for burnin.' Given that western society treats art and artefacts with a kind of religious reverence, the notion that they ought to be burnt – even if expressed in jest – is deeply irreverent and even profane.[6]**
>
> **Finally, this vignette portrays Mrs Flushing as overbearing – as someone who enjoys dominating and steering the conversation.[7] A particularly telling exchange comes near the end of the extract: Mrs Flushing posits a peculiar, attention-seeking question ('What would you do if spiders came out of the tap...?'), and not only demands an answer (the word 'demanded' is used twice), but also, before Mrs. Ambrose can do anything more than shrug and 'smile,' simply continues to hold court.[8]**

The mark scheme for this will not contain an exhaustive list of adjectives you can use. Instead, the examiner will be looking for any three adjectives that work, combined with a mature explanation of the reasoning behind your choice.

3. This question tests your understanding of character. Think about the character of Mrs. Thornbury. In your own words, explain what the following two quotations say about her character:

a) Mrs. Thornbury acted as interpreter, making things smooth all round by a series of charming commonplace remarks. [3]

That Thornbury acts to ease the flow and coherency of conversation (that is, instead of trying to insert her personality into proceedings), indicates that she is a kind of social matchmaker: an individual who feels a need to help social relationships flourish, and to generally try and make conversation more enjoyable and amiable. Indeed, the implication is that when she does speak, it is intended chiefly to induce pleasure in her interlocutors, whereas the actual substance of her words is perhaps somewhat inconsequential and ancillary.[9]

The examiner is looking for the candidate to acknowledge the fact that Mrs. Thornbury is an individual who aims to create social relationships between people she knows – and doing so would win the first mark. The second mark is for acknowledging that, in conversation, Mrs. Thornbury works to make things as pleasurable as possible for the participants.

The third mark for this particular question is likely set aside for the overall flair and sophistication of your answer.

b) "'I've taken it upon myself, Mr. Ambrose," she said, "to promise that you will be so kind as to give Mrs. Flushing the benefit of your experience.'" [3]

By making commitments on other people's behalf, Mrs. Thornbury demonstrates a willingness to impose on one party in order to try and artificially engineer a relationship between two separate parties: a trait that demonstrates a degree of audacity, but also her passion for social matchmaking. That she resorts to flattery to smooth the way with the party on whom she is imposing not only points to her desire to please her interlocutors, but also points to a subtle cunning in her makeup: she is, after all, manipulating Mr Ambrose in this instance.

The first mark is for acknowledging that this quote reveals a tendency in Mrs Flushing's personality to impose on others when she feels it will further her social matchmaking aims. The second mark is for discussing the implications of her use of flattery. Again, the third mark is for expressing these points with flair.

4. This question tests your ability to explain the meanings of words as they appear in the passage. Work out the meaning of the following words based on their meaning in the passage. [6]

a) Splendidly (line 8)

Splendidly here means wonderfully.

b) Carriage (line 8)

Carriage here means posture.

c) Encyclopaedic (line 18)

Encyclopaedic here mean extensive.

d) Eccentric (line 29)

Eccentric here means idiosyncratic.

e) Disapproval (line 42)

Disapproval here means condemnation.

f) Intervened (line 46)

Intervened here means interjected.

5. This question tests your ability to find a quotation and explain its meaning.

a) Mrs Ambrose's husband, Ridley, is present throughout the passage. Using a quotation to back up your view, what do you think his job might be?

QUOTATION [1]

'...my husband spends his life in digging up manuscripts which nobody wants.'

EXPLANATION [3]

I believe that Ridley is likely to be an academic of some kind. That he spends 'his life...digging up manuscripts' suggests that this pursuit is likely his job; and given that the comment comes shortly after Mrs. Flushing bemoans all things old, the insinuation is that the manuscripts Ridley deals with are old. Professions that involve digging up manuscripts are not multitudinous, but academia would be among them:

he could perhaps be a historian, investigating manuscripts of a certain era, or a literature academic.[10] **While it is possible that he might instead be a collector or an antiques dealer, it seems likely the narrator would have spelt this out when the topic of Mr. Flushing (who is identified as a collector) arose.**

The above quotation is the one the examiner is looking for: indeed, it is the only one that really gives us a substantial indication of what Ridley does for a living.

Insofar as the explanation is concerned, any answer that the student can convincingly link to the studying of 'manuscripts' – particularly old ones – will be credited, and the rest of the marks are for the strength of the student's reasoning. You will notice that I in fact mention other professions that might also have been plausible, thereby alerting the examiner to my appreciation of other possibilities.

6. This question tests your ability to explain the meanings of quotations. In your own words, and based on the context of the passage, explain why the writer has written the following:

a) "What would you do if spiders came out of the tap when you turned on the hot water?" [3]

The writer, by having Mrs. Flushing follow up on her claim for why she does not like large houses with this hyperbolic and absurd image, is attempting to convey Mrs. Flushing's hyperbolic and histrionic manner of conversation: she is a larger-than-life character who likes to shock and entertain with her conversation.[11] **The writer is also conveying Mrs. Flushing's privilege: she has the ways and means to be able to not only choose to live in a large house, but also to refuse to live in a large house. The writer includes this comment also as a means to reveal the character of the individuals with whom Mrs. Flushing is conversing through their reactions.**

Again, we have been asked to write in our own words for these questions, so please ensure that you do so.

The marks here are available for discussing the ways the author includes this quote to further Mrs. Flushing's personality and background: for instance, the fact it reveals her tendency towards histrionics, or extreme privilege (to score both marks, you'll need to have some sophistication to your response).

The third mark is for acknowledging that the author includes this comment as a way to reveal the personalities of other characters.

b) 'Mrs. Ambrose shrugged her shoulders with a smile.' [2]

> **Mrs. Ambrose's seemingly passive response to Mrs. Flushing's outlandish comment – a response that answers only with a piece of noncommittal body-language – is a way for the writer not only to convey the overbearing impact Mrs. Flushing has on others, but also perhaps to capture a passivity in Mrs. Ambrose's character.[12] That said, one might argue that the writer has written this to portray Mrs Ambrose not as a passive individual, but as a patient individual: someone willing to humour the absurdities of others in the name of social nicety.**

One mark is available for discussing how the writer includes this quote to further reveal the effect of Mrs. Flushing's words upon others. The second mark is for a mature comment on how the writer reveals more about Mrs. Ambrose's personality with this quote – they could argue, for instance, that it reveals a passivity, or that it reveals that Mrs. Ambrose is someone who is happy to humour others.

c) 'Ridley sighed that he never expected any one to understand anything, least of all politicians.' [3]

> **The author includes this detail of Ridley's reaction to Mrs. flushing's comment to give an insight into his personality, though the insight is enigmatic: on one hand, he could be earnestly agreeing with Mrs Flushing's somewhat absurd comment regarding a politician; on the other, he could be speaking with some irony, and mocking this swipe at a politician. At any rate, the author also writes this as a means of reminding the audience of Ridley's hitherto quiet presence, and to draw retrospective attention to the fact that he had not as yet spoken in the conversation (and in fact even here his words are not recorded verbatim, almost as if Ridley is muted even as he speaks).[13]**

One mark is reserved for understanding that the author uses this quote to draw attention to Ridley's silence up to this point.

The candidate can earn a second point by observing that the author does not quote Ridley directly (although she does record the other characters verbatim), which works to sideline his voice further. Yet even if the candidate does not make this observation, they can score the two further marks anyway with comments exploring how the writer includes this quote to reveal aspects of Ridley's personality, with each mature point of this kind being worth one mark apiece.

Line By Line Papers

Note: This style of paper has more in common with the Close Language Paper than it does the All Rounder Paper, because, like the Close Language Paper, much of the paper is comprised of low-scoring, quick-fire questions. That said, there is a 'mini essay' style question right at the end of this paper, which is reminiscent of the longer questions in the All Rounder Paper.

As you'll be able to see – and as the name suggests – the paper goes through the extract in a linear fashion. The most popular types of questions in this paper are those that require us to sleuth out answers, and those that ask us to explain things in our own words.

Both of the Line By Line papers I've included here are out of a total of thirty-five marks.

This extract is taken from a novel set in nineteenth century America. This extract dramatises Jo and her friend Laurie's ice-skating expedition along a frozen river, and the action that ensues as Jo's younger sister, Amy, attempts to join them.

1   It was not far to the river, but both were ready before Amy reached them. Jo saw her coming, and turned her back. Laurie did not see, for he was carefully skating along the shore, sounding the ice, for a warm spell had preceded the cold snap.

   "I'll go on to the first bend, and see if it's all right before we begin to race," Amy
5   heard him say, as he shot away, looking like a young Russian in his fur-trimmed coat and cap.

   Jo heard Amy panting after her run, stamping her feet and blowing on her fingers as she tried to put her skates on, but Jo never turned and went slowly zigzagging down the river, taking a bitter, unhappy sort of satisfaction in her sister's troubles. She had
10   cherished her anger till it grew strong and took possession of her, as evil thoughts and feelings always do unless cast out at once. As Laurie turned the bend, he shouted back...

   "Keep near the shore. It isn't safe in the middle." Jo heard, but Amy was struggling to her feet and did not catch a word. Jo glanced over her shoulder, and the little demon
15   she was harboring said in her ear...

"No matter whether she heard or not, let her take care of herself."

Laurie had vanished round the bend, Jo was just at the turn, and Amy, far behind, striking out toward the smoother ice in the middle of the river. For a minute Jo stood still with a strange feeling in her heart, then she resolved to go on, but something held
20   and turned her round, just in time to see Amy throw up her hands and go down, with a sudden crash of rotten ice, the splash of water, and a cry that made Jo's heart stand still with fear. She tried to call Laurie, but her voice was gone. She tried to rush forward, but her feet seemed to have no strength in them, and for a second, she could only stand motionless, staring with a terror-stricken face at the little blue hood above
25   the black water. Something rushed swiftly by her, and Laurie's voice cried out...

"Bring a rail. Quick, quick!"

How she did it, she never knew, but for the next few minutes she worked as if possessed, blindly obeying Laurie, who was quite self-possessed, and lying flat, held Amy up by his arm and hockey stick till Jo dragged a rail from the fence, and together
30   they got the child out, more frightened than hurt.

"Now then, we must walk her home as fast as we can. Pile our things on her, while I get off these confounded skates," cried Laurie, wrapping his coat round Amy, and tugging away at the straps which never seemed so intricate before.

Shivering, dripping, and crying, they got Amy home, and after an exciting time of it,
35   she fell asleep, rolled in blankets before a hot fire. During the bustle Jo had scarcely spoken but flown about, looking pale and wild, with her things half off, her dress torn, and her hands cut and bruised by ice and rails and refractory buckles. When Amy was comfortably asleep, the house quiet, and Mrs. March sitting by the bed, she called Jo to her and began to bind up the hurt hands.

40   "Are you sure she is safe?" whispered Jo, looking remorsefully at the golden head, which might have been swept away from her sight forever under the treacherous ice.

"Quite safe, dear. She is not hurt, and won't even take cold, I think, you were so sensible in covering and getting her home quickly," replied her mother cheerfully.

"Laurie did it all. I only let her go. Mother, if she should die, it would be my fault."
45   And Jo dropped down beside the bed in a passion of penitent tears, telling all that had happened, bitterly condemning her hardness of heart, and sobbing out her gratitude for being spared the heavy punishment which might have come upon her.

"It's my dreadful temper! I try to cure it, I think I have, and then it breaks out worse than ever. Oh, Mother, what shall I do? What shall I do?" cried poor Jo, in despair.

50   "Watch and pray, dear, never get tired of trying, and never think it is impossible to conquer your fault," said Mrs. March, drawing the blowzy head to her shoulder and kissing the wet cheek so tenderly that Jo cried even harder.

An extract from Louisa May Alcott's Little Women

---

1. Lines 1-3

Why does Laurie not see Amy when she arrives at the riverbank? [1]

2. In your own words, explain why Laurie feels the need to sound the ice [2]

3. Lines 9-10

Explain what is meant by the following: 'She had cherished her anger till it grew strong and took possession of her.' [2]

4. Lines 13-16

In your own words, explain why Jo does not repeat Laurie's warning to Amy. [2]

5. Lines 17-28

In your own words, explain the meaning of the following:

a) '...she resolved to go on, but something held and turned her round' [2]

b) '...for the next few minutes she worked as if possessed, blindly obeying Laurie.' [2]

6. After Amy has fallen through the ice, but before Laurie intervenes, what two things does Jo try and fail to do in order to help? [2]

7. Lines 28-30

How do Laurie and Jo fish Amy out of the water? Identify three details [3]

8. Lines 40-41

At lines 40 to 41 it notes that Jo is seen '...looking remorsefully at the golden head, which might have been swept away from her sight for ever under the treacherous ice.' What does this mean? [2]

9. Lines 30-42

How do we know that Amy is not physically hurt after she is retrieved from the water? Looking at lines 30-42, find two phrases that tell you this. [4]

10. Lines 46-47

At lines 46-47, the author describes Jo as 'sobbing out her gratitude for being spared the heavy punishment which might have come upon her'? Explain what you think this could mean. [3]

11. Lines 50-51

Between lines 50-51, what rationale does Mrs March offer Jo for continuing to work on her temper? [2]

12. Using the whole passage, explain how the writer uses language to make this sequence exciting. Use short quotations to support your answer. [8]

Paper Five: Model Answers & Guidance

1. Lines 1-3

Why does Laurie not see Amy when she arrives at the riverbank? [1]

Laurie does not see Amy as she arrives because he has already started skating along the river.

You need to have the answer I've given above to secure this mark (or words to the same effect). It is simply a case of reading the passage carefully. However, you'll notice that the examiner has prefaced the question with an indication of where within the passage the answer will be located. Be sure to pay close attention to clues of this kind.

Notice also that my answer is a full sentence. As mentioned elsewhere, we should only dispense with full sentences when given explicit permission to do so.

2. In your own words, explain why Laurie feels the need to sound the ice [2]

Laurie felt compelled to check the ice's integrity due to the weather conditions that preceded their expedition: although the temperature had very recently dropped and caused the river water to freeze, it had just beforehand been fairly warm, and thus Laurie is wary that, as a result of

this prior warmth, the top layer of ice may not be thick enough to hold their weight.

One mark is for acknowledging the weather conditions: the warm weather that had come just prior to the cold. The second is to discussing why the warm weather causes Laurie to proceed with caution: namely, the fact that these conditions might have compromised the integrity of the ice.

3. Lines 9-10

Explain what is meant by the following: 'She had cherished her anger till it grew strong and took possession of her.' [2]

The idea that Jo has 'cherished her anger' implies that, instead of identifying her anger as something negative and combating it, Jo has instead indulged her feelings of anger against her sister, thereby allowing these feelings to thrive. By stating that Jo's anger 'took possession of her,' the writer personifies anger as something that has usurped Jo's agency, thereby communicating the fact that this emotion has become her prime motivation.[1]

The first mark is for dissecting the phrase 'cherished her anger,' and for demonstrating an understanding that this means that Jo was actively indulging her anger. The second mark is for dissecting the idea that it 'took possession of her,' and how this suggests that her anger seems almost to have overridden Jo's free will.

4. Lines 13-16

In your own words, explain why Jo does not repeat Laurie's warning to Amy. [2]

It appears that Jo's chief motivation for not repeating Laurie's warning to Amy is the anger she feels for her sister, which seems to induce in Jo a sense of vindictiveness; a mentality that Amy does not deserve the luxury of hearing Laurie's warning regarding the ice's integrity, and ought to be left instead to fend for herself.

The first mark is for identifying Jo's anger as the chief motivating factor for her behaviour. A second mark is for acknowledging that Jo wants Amy to be forced to fend for herself.

5. Lines 17-28

In your own words, explain the meaning of the following:

a) '...she resolved to go on, but something held and turned her round' [2]

That Jo decides to push forward, yet in fact remains fixed to the spot and turns around, appears to indicate that Jo is experiencing an inner conflict: whereas her conscious train of thought is chiefly animated by an anger and vindictiveness that wishes to punish her sister, it is being tempered by a unconscious force – perhaps her moral compass; perhaps her latent love for her sister – that prevents Jo from abandoning her sister altogether, and in fact induces Jo to check on her sister's wellbeing.

The first mark here is for articulating that Jo is experiencing an inner conflict, though candidates do not need to use that exact phraseology: they may perhaps say that Jo's emotions are pulling her two ways, or that she is emotionally torn. So long as the idea of inner conflict is adequately expressed, however, the candidate will score this first mark.

The second mark is for articulating the nature of that inner conflict: on the one hand, she is angry with her sister and wishes to punish her. On the other, she loves her sister, and does not wish her to come to serious harm.

b) '...for the next few minutes she worked as if possessed, blindly obeying Laurie.' [2]

The conceit of possession does not on this occasion imply that Jo was motivated by anger, but instead implies that Jo is working with an almost supernatural energy and intensity: that is, she is working as if an otherworldly entity has taken possession of her body, affording her supernatural strength and persistence. As she does so, the writer does not wish us to believe that she is literally unable to see, but rather that she is following Laurie's instructions unquestioningly, and is thus figuratively blind to any distractions.

The tricky thing here is that the author once again deploys the idea of being 'possessed,' yet on this occasion uses it in a slightly different way.

At any rate, the candidate must be able to convey that, by saying that Jo worked 'as if possessed,' the writer is conveying that Jo is working as though her body had been taken over by some supernatural entity. A second mark is available for articulating the fact that Jo is not literally in a state of blindness as she obeys Laurie – rather, that the phrase is used to express how single-mindedly she is adhering to Laurie's instructions.

6. After Amy has fallen through the ice, but before Laurie intervenes, what two things does Jo try and fail to do in order to help? [2]

> **Jo, in order to try and help her sister, tries first to call out to Laurie and raise the alarm. Failing that, Jo next attempts to move towards her sister, though fails to galvanise herself into motion.**

To score both marks here, you need to identify these two points: a) Jo tries to shout out for help; and b) Jo tries to move towards her sister.

7. Lines 28-30

How do Laurie and Jo fish Amy out of the water? Identify three details [3]

> **Laurie and Jo fish Amy out of the water with a two-pronged approach: while Laurie kept Amy afloat with his 'arm' and 'hockey stick,' Jo fetched a rail that had belonged to a 'fence,' and one can infer the rail was then used to give Amy something more substantial to latch onto, and was used to heave her out the water**

The three details the examiners are looking for you to mention are Laurie's arm, his hockey-stick, and the rail Jo fetches.

8. Lines 40-41

At lines 40 to 41 it notes that Jo is seen '...looking remorsefully at the golden head, which might have been swept away from her sight for ever under the treacherous ice.' What does this mean? [2]

> **The 'golden head' refers to Amy's blonde hair: Jo is looking at Amy with remorse because she feels guilty for not having warned Amy about the dangers the ice had presented – dangers that might have led to Amy's**

death. Indeed, the idea that Amy would 'have been swept away from [Jo] sight for ever' is a euphemistic recognition that the event might have been fatal.

I am scoring my first mark by pointing out that the 'golden head' is referring to the fact that Jo can see the blonde hair atop Amy's head. I secure my second by discussing how 'swept away for ever' is an expression that telegraphs that Jo understands the extreme, even deadly, nature of the danger afoot.

You will also notice that I make a third point that sees me discuss the word 'remorsefully,' and what this tells us about Jo's feelings towards the unfolding disaster. This is an example of me going 'the extra mile,' and giving the examiner no room to dock me a mark!

9. Lines 30-42

How do we know that Amy is not physically hurt after she is retrieved from the water? Looking at lines 30-42, find two phrases that tell you this. [4]

> **'...together they got the child out, more frightened than hurt.'**
>
> **'..."she is not hurt, and won't even take cold."'**

The above two quotes are by far and away the best ones to pick out, and will be certain to score you two marks apiece.

If a candidate picks out the phrase 'Amy was comfortably asleep,' they would likely score a single mark, since, while not as explicit, the word 'comfortably' strongly hints that Amy had not been badly hurt.

10. Lines 46-47

At lines 46-47, the author describes Jo as 'sobbing out her gratitude for being spared the heavy punishment which might have come upon her'? Explain what you think this could mean. [3]

> **The author is suggesting that Jo is overcome with relief by the fact that she had not been punished for her cruelty and negligence with the loss of her sister. The image of her 'crying out her gratitude' not only indicates that she is crying in thankfulness that her sister had survived, but the image itself seems to almost suggest that the tears are a physical**

manifestation of gratitude. Moreover, the lexicon of thankfulness ('gratitude') and retribution ('heavy punishment') seems to give this almost a prayerful quality: it appears to suggest that Jo construes of her transgression as a religious crime, and that she had been 'spared' by some deity that might have seen fit to punish her.[2]

Two marks are reserved for demonstrating an understanding that this quote indicates that Jo is overwhelmed with relief because she had dodged a catastrophe (losing her sister). The third mark is for adding an extra level of sophistication to your answer: perhaps an observation regarding how Jo's tears become symbolic of her gratitude, or the fact that the quote, with its prayerful quality, seems to hint that Jo believes she has been on the receiving end of something akin to divine mercy.

As ever, I have gone above and beyond and made both of these observation; though I likely would have scored all three marks even without my closing sentence.

11. Lines 50-51

Between lines 50-51, what rationale does Mrs March offer Jo for continuing to work on her temper? [2]

> **Mrs March argues that Jo ought to continue working on her temper because it is possible to change and improve ourselves, and thus working on oneself is always worthwhile: as Mrs March puts it, 'never think it is impossible to conquer your fault.'**

One mark is reserved for correctly identifying the rationale Mrs March offers Jo for continuing to work on her temper – namely, that it is always possible to improve oneself. To score the second mark, the candidate needs to include a snippet of evidence from the extract.

12. Using the whole passage, explain how the writer uses language to make this sequence exciting. Use short quotations to support your answer. [8]

> **One of the central sources of excitement in this extract is the emphasis on physical motion as the events unfold. The opening paragraph has Amy approaching the riverside – 'Jo saw her coming' – and the reader learns shortly after she had in fact been running ('panting after her run'). Laurie is seemingly in perpetual motion: he is first 'carefully skating;' next, he has 'shot away' – a turn of phrase metaphorically likening his**

motion to that of a gunshot; and, after Amy's fall, Laurie moves past Jo at such a pace that Jo does not even register who it is: 'something rushed swiftly by [Jo].' Indeed, when Laurie speaks, it is to urge even greater speed: 'Quick, quick!' Jo herself is 'zigzagging down the river' early on, is later seen rushing to grab a fence rail, and maintains her high tempo back at home: 'Jo had...flown about... with her things half off.' This emphasis on the language of kinesis imbues the whole sequence with a sense of breathlessness and excitement.[3]

Also powerful in generating excitement is the author's skill in building anticipation. The mere mention that Laurie is 'sounding the ice' functions as something akin to a Chekov's gun: once the danger the ice represents has been mentioned, there is a tacit expectation it will come into play.[4] The writer continues to titillate with this sense of danger, most noticeably via Laurie's exhortation that 'it isn't safe in the middle' of the river – the phrase 'isn't safe' again reminding the reader of the latent peril – while the narrator's observation shortly afterwards that Amy has struck 'out towards...the middle of the river' only ratchets up the morbid excitement further. Yet if mentions of the unsafe central reservation build excitement, so too does Jo's uncanny sense of foreboding: both the 'strange feeling at her heart,' as well as the intuition that 'turned her around,' combine to thrill the reader with a sense of impending doom.

Excitement also stems from the sheer intensity of Jo's emotions. Her anger with her sister, and her seeming capacity to do her harm, is exciting in its own right. The conceit of the 'little demon' in Jo's 'ear' engagingly brings to life Jo's vindictiveness, while the inner struggle she then endures as her vindictiveness and conscience duke it out is exciting insofar as it represents a struggle between good and evil: as Jo finds herself standing 'still, with a strange feeling at her heart,' so too does the reader find their own hearts struck as they vicariously experience Jo's struggle. However, if this inner struggle is exciting, perhaps even more so is Jo's fear once Amy plummets: a fear so intense that it temporarily renders Jo mute ('her voice was gone'), and paralysed: 'her feet seemed to have no strength.'

After a litany of quick-fire questions, this paper ends with a 'mini essay' type question, reminiscent of the ones we saw in the All Rounder Paper.

A key difference to the mini essays we saw in the All Rounder Paper is that this question is asking us to focus explicitly on '*how the writer uses language*.' So whereas in the All Rounder Paper we had room to discuss things like free indirect style, this time we want to be laser-focused on just the language.

Of course, eight marks does not mean you need eight separate points. On the contrary, my tactic above has been to make three strong points, and to write each with enough detail to ensure that each paragraph is worth three marks (yes, I know the marks for this question is capped at eight – but my mentality is to ensure that I am giving the examiner no excuse not to award me full marks).

As ever, I put together a short plan before I started writing.

- The speed and kinesis with which the children move as events unfold
- An air of anticipation: not only by referring the danger presented by the ice right at the beginning, but also through Jo's uncanny sense of foreboding.
- The sheer intensity of Jo's emotion all the way through: be it her vindictiveness, her fear, her penitence.

As I have mentioned in the foreword, there are often alternative points that a candidate might discuss that would also be worthy of scoring marks. To illustrate, I'll add another couple of paragraphs below that would also answer the question, and which I would imagine might both be worth two or three marks apiece:

The author achieves further excitement by prolonging the sense of danger: not only does Amy's fall itself represent danger, but the danger persists even once she is fished out, for she is dangerously cold. Laurie's tone remains fraught even once Amy has been retrieved ('cried Laurie'), and he instructs Jo to wrap Amy up amid a general atmosphere of freneticism: Laurie is somehow 'wrapping his coat around Amy' and 'tugging away' at his skate straps all at once. [5] That the author explicitly refers to the interim between Amy arriving home and her winding up in bed as 'an exciting time' leaves no ambiguity as to the effect she is attempting to achieve.

It might be argued, finally, that the calm that reigns later in the extract, as the focus shifts to the slow-paced domestic setting, functions to heighten the previous drama and excitement in retrospect through the force of juxtaposition. [6] Whereas the extract starts with running and skating and danger, the domestic realm is characterised by comfort and safety: the reader is told Amy is 'comfortably asleep' – the adverb 'comfortably' emphasising that the distress has passed – and 'the house was quiet,' the silence a kind of shorthand for a lack of drama. Yet while

the calm functions to sharpen the prior excitement, one might also note that Jo's emotions are still greatly heightened during this domestic sequence as she grapples with her guilt, and this arguably remains a source of excitement in its own right. Indeed, the final line specifies 'that Jo cried even harder,' suggesting excess upon excess.

This is an extract from a novel set in Chicago, USA, in the late nineteenth century. This passage recounts Carrie's experiences as she attends her first day at work.

1 Once in the sunlit street, with labourers tramping by in either direction, the horse-cars passing crowded to the rails with the small clerks and floor help in the great wholesale houses, and men and women generally coming out of doors and passing about the neighbourhood, Carrie felt slightly reassured. In the sunshine of the morn-
5 ing, beneath the wide, blue heavens, with a fresh wind astir, what fears, except the most desperate, can find a harbourage? In the night, or the gloomy chambers of the day, fears and misgivings wax strong, but out in the sunlight there is, for a time, cessation even of the terror of death.

Carrie went straight forward until she crossed the river, and then turned into Fifth
10 Avenue. The thoroughfare, in this part, was like a walled canon of brown stone and dark red brick. The big windows looked shiny and clean. Trucks were rumbling in increasing numbers; men and women, girls and boys were moving onward in all directions. She met girls of her own age, who looked at her as if with contempt for her diffidence. She wondered at the magnitude of this life and at the importance of
15 knowing much in order to do anything in it at all. Dread at her own inefficiency crept upon her. She would not know how, she would not be quick enough. Had not all the other places refused her because she did not know something or other? She would be scolded, abused, ignominiously discharged.

It was with weak knees and a slight catch in her breathing that she came up to the
20 great shoe company at Adams and Fifth Avenue and entered the elevator. When she
stepped out on the fourth floor there was no one at hand, only great aisles of boxes
piled to the ceiling. She stood, very much frightened, awaiting some one.

Presently Mr. Brown came up. He did not seem to recognise her.

"What is it you want?" he inquired.

25 Carrie's heart sank.

"You said I should come this morning to see about work—"

"Oh," he interrupted. "Um—yes. What is your name?"

"Carrie Meeber."

"Yes," said he. "You come with me."

30 He led the way through dark, box-lined aisles which had the smell of new shoes, until
they came to an iron door which opened into the factory proper. There was a large,
low-ceiled room, with clacking, rattling machines at which men in white shirt sleeves
and blue gingham aprons were working. She followed him diffidently through the
clattering automatons, keeping her eyes straight before her, and flushing slightly. They
35 crossed to a far corner and took an elevator to the sixth floor. Out of the array of
machines and benches, Mr. Brown signalled a foreman.

"This is the girl," he said, and turning to Carrie, "You go with him." He then
returned, and Carrie followed her new superior to a little desk in a corner, which he
used as a kind of official centre.

40 "You've never worked at anything like this before, have you?" he questioned, rather
sternly.

"No, sir," she answered.

He seemed rather annoyed at having to bother with such help, but put down her
name and then led her across to where a line of girls occupied stools in front of
45 clacking machines. On the shoulder of one of the girls who was punching eye-holes
in one piece of the upper, by the aid of the machine, he put his hand.

"You," he said, "show this girl how to do what you're doing. When you get through,
come to me."

The girl so addressed rose promptly and gave Carrie her place.

50 "It isn't hard to do," she said, bending over. "You just take this so, fasten it with this
clamp, and start the machine."

She suited action to word, fastened the piece of leather, which was eventually to form the right half of the upper of a man's shoe, by little adjustable clamps, and pushed a small steel rod at the side of the machine. The latter jumped to the task of punching,
55 with sharp, snapping clicks, cutting circular bits of leather out of the side of the upper, leaving the holes which were to hold the laces. After observing a few times, the girl let her work at it alone. Seeing that it was fairly well done, she went away.

The pieces of leather came from the girl at the machine to her right, and were passed on to the girl at her left. Carrie saw at once that an average speed was necessary or
60 the work would pile up on her and all those below would be delayed. She had no time to look about, and bent anxiously to her task. The girls at her left and right realised her predicament and feelings, and, in a way, tried to aid her, as much as they dared, by working slower.

An extract from Theodore Dreiser's Sister Carrie

1. Lines 1-8

Identify three separate types of people Carrie spots on the thoroughfare she walks along prior to crossing the river. [3]

2. Explain what is meant by the following: '...out in the sunlight there is, for a time, cessation even of the terror of death.' [3]

3. Lines 9-10

What road does Carrie turn onto after crossing the river? [1]

4. Lines 13-15

In your own words, explain the meaning of the following:

a) 'She met girls of her own age, who looked at her as if with contempt for her diffidence' [2]

b) She wondered at the magnitude of this life and at the importance of knowing much in order to do anything in it at all. [2]

5. Lines 15-18

In your own words, summarise the reason that Carrie cites for believing she is unlikely to do well in her new job. [2]

6. Lines 19-23

Look again at lines 19-23, which recount Carrie's arrival outside the shoe factory and her meeting with Mr Brown on the fourth floor. Find two phrases that suggest (either explicitly or implicitly) that Carrie is in a state of distress. [4]

7. Lines 30-34

Identify the two types of room Carrie encounters on the fourth floor [2]

8. Lines 37-43

Between lines 37-43, what is it that elicits irritation in the foreman? [2]

9. Line 52

At line 52, it says: 'She suited action to word.' What does this mean? [2]

10. Lines 52-57

In your own words, explain why the woman introduced to Carrie by the foreman eventually decides to leave Carrie unattended. [2]

11. Lines 61-63

At lines 61 to 63 it says 'The girls at her left and right realised her predicament and feelings, and, in a way, tried to aid her, as much as they dared, by working slower.' Explain what you think this could mean. [2]

12. Using the whole passage, explain how the writer uses language to make Carrie's experience attending her first day at work seem intimidating. Use short quotations to support your answer. [8]

1. Lines 1-8

Identify three separate types of people Carrie spots on the thoroughfare she walks along prior to crossing the river. [3]

Before crossing the river, Carrie spots labourers, clerks, and the floor staff from wholesale houses.

If you mentioned the 'men and women generally coming out doors' in lieu of one of the above, you would still be eligible for a mark.

Given the way the first sentence to this extract is written, it is ambiguous whether the 'small clerks' Carrie spots also work at the 'great wholesale houses' with the 'floor help.' In any case, if a student cites the clerks, they will get the mark regardless of whether they identify them as working at the great wholesale houses or not.

2. Explain what is meant by the following: '...out in the sunlight there is, for a time, cessation even of the terror of death.' [3]

This quote gives an insight into Carrie's contemplations, and articulates her sense that, in comparison to how darkness seems to encourage dark thoughts, 'in the sunlight' people no longer register a sense of fear at the prospect of dying. There appears to be a crucial sense of temporality,

however, to this respite from the fear of mortality: the 'cessation' – which means a stopping or pausing – can only last 'for a time,' thereby implying that these fears will re-emerge once darkness regains ascendancy.[1]

This is a tricky question, because so much hinges on knowing the meaning of the word 'cessation.' That said, if you don't know the meaning of a word like this, don't throw in the towel. Instead, read the sentences either side of it very carefully, because it may be possible to infer the meaning from the context.

Two marks can be earned for coherently explaining that the quote captures Carrie's sense that the sunlight causes people to stop fearing death. The final mark depends on recognising the temporality of this dissipation of fear, as indicated by the expression 'for a time.'

3. Lines 9-10

What road does Carrie turn onto after crossing the river? [1]

After crossing the river, Carrie turns onto Fifth Avenue.

Students will only be awarded the mark if they cite Fifth Avenue.

4. Lines 13-15

In your own words, explain the meaning of the following:

a) 'She met girls of her own age, who looked at her as if with contempt for her diffidence' [2]

This quote indicates that Carrie, as she commuted by foot, passed by a number of young women of a similar age to herself, and that Carrie felt not only as though these women could divine her meekness, but also that these women's expressions as they laid eyes on her indicated a disdain for her meekness.

The two marks available are for demonstrating an understanding that: a) the women Carrie encounters seem to look at her with contempt/disdain; and b) their contempt appears to stem from having intuited Carrie's weakness/diffidence (though, of course, the student needs to be explaining all of this in their own words).

b) <u>She wondered at the magnitude of this life and at the importance of knowing much in order to do anything in it at all.</u> [2]

> **This sentence indicates that Carrie was meditating on the enormity of existence, though there is ambiguity with regards to what precisely she considers enormous – whether Carrie construes the universe as physically enormous, whether she believes there is enormous significance in merely being alive, or whether she feels the enormity resides in the impact (be it emotional, psychological, or otherwise) existence has on the individual. Either way, Carrie's key takeaway appears to be a belief that, given this enormity, an individual must accumulate great knowledge to lead an impactful life.**

The two marks available are for demonstrating an understanding that: a) Carrie is overwhelmed by the sheer enormity of life; and b) her sense of being overwhelmed induces in her a conviction that only through accumulating great knowledge might an individual have an impact.

You will notice that not only do I acknowledge the vagueness of the phrase 'magnitude of life,' but that I also explore how the author's choice to leave things ambiguous impacts on meaning. It is possible that a strict examiner might even cap students who fail to acknowledge this ambiguity to one mark, since it is a crucial facet of this sentence.

5. Lines 15-18

<u>In your own words, summarise the reason that Carrie cites for believing she is unlikely to do well in her new job.</u> [2]

> **Carrie's belief that she will fail in her new job derives from a conviction that she lacks pre-existing skills and knowledge, and that she lacks also the capacity to pick up these skills and knowledge with sufficient speed. To support this mentality, Carrie draws on her experience interacting with previous employers, all of whom had cited her gaps in knowledge when opting to turn her down.**

The examiner is looking for two specific points here to award the marks: a) Carrie's belief that she lacks the skills and knowledge to succeed in her new job; and b) that this was compounded by the fact that Carrie, when being sacked from previous positions, had been told she had lacked the requisite knowledge.[2]

6. Lines 19-23

Look again at lines 19-23, which recount Carrie's arrival outside the shoe factory and her meeting with Mr Brown on the fourth floor. Find two phrases that suggest (either explicitly or implicitly) that Carrie is in a state of distress. [4]

> **'It was with weak knees and a slight catch in her breathing...'**
>
> **'She stood, very much frightened...'**

Given that the question suggests you can use either explicit or implicit evidence, we can take this as a clue that there is a chance that only one quote in the passage we have been told to look at will explicitly spell out Carrie's sense of distress, and that we may need to find a second quote that points to her stress more tacitly.

Sure enough, looking at lines 19-23, this is the case. The second quote I've offered above, via the word 'frightened,' gives an explicit indication that Carrie is in a state of distress. However, the first quote I've included conveys her distress tacitly through body language that we would usually associate with someone being in distress.

7. Lines 30-34

Identify the two types of room Carrie encounters on the fourth floor [2]

> **On the fourth floor, Carrie encounters first a shoe storage room, full of 'box-lined aisles,' and then a factory, in which various machines are being operated.**

One mark is at stake for each correctly identified room.

8. Lines 37-43

Between lines 37-43, what is it that elicits irritation in the foreman? [2]

> **The foreman is irritated because he learns that Carrie has no experience in the type of manufacturing work he oversees, and feels put-upon at having to make do with inexperienced new employees such as Carrie.**

Crucial here is to display an understanding that the foreman is frustrated at Carrie's lack of experience. To pick up the second mark, however, you need to have linked Carrie's lack of experience to the foreman's workload: he believes it will make his life harder.

9. Line 52

At lines 52, it says: 'She suited action to word.' What does this mean? [2]

> **This expression suggests that the woman aiding Carrie, who at this point in the extract has just described to Carrie how to use the machine she had been using when Carrie arrived, makes good on these instructions (which the narrator refers to as her 'word') by giving Carrie a demonstration (that is, the woman puts her 'word' into 'action').**

This is a particularly devilish question, as the word 'she' here is ambiguous: is it the unnamed worker suiting 'action to word' or Carrie? The answer is in fact further along in the paragraph: we learn at lines 56-57 that 'the girl let her work at it alone,' which implies that the unnamed woman had been the one working the machine up to that point.

To get the two marks here, the student must not only recognise that the unnamed woman is the one suiting 'action to word,' but that this expression indicates that the unnamed woman first explained how to use the machine, and then demonstrated doing so for Carrie.

Be aware that on this occasion we have not been asked to use our own words. As a result, we are allowed to use short quotes to help us answer the question.

10. Lines 52-57

In your own words, explain why the woman introduced to Carrie by the foreman eventually decides to leave Carrie unattended. [2]

> **The woman instructing Carrie finally leaves Carrie to work on the machine alone because, after demonstrating to Carrie how to operate the machine, and then repeatedly watching Carrie successfully puncture holes in the leather, she had surmised that Carrie had sufficiently come to grips with the skill. Given that the foreman had instructed the woman to seek him out once she had brought Carrie up to speed, and it had become clear that Carrie could now operate the machine with a basic**

level of competence, the woman had decided she had completed the task the foreman had set, and thus departed to seek him out.

The two points you need to cover here – each worth one mark apiece – are as follows: a) the woman could see that Carrie had reached a basic level of competency; and b) she had been asked to find the foreman after she completed her task.

11. Lines 61-63

At lines 61 to 63 it says 'The girls at her left and right realised her predicament and feelings, and, in a way, tried to aid her, as much as they dared, by working slower.' Explain what you think this could mean. [2]

The women working either side of Carrie discern that Carrie is facing a 'predicament' as a result of her pace of work: because she is inexperienced and unable to match their pace, she is at risk of creating a backlog and slowing down those individuals further along the chain of production – an issue that that would not only hamper productivity, but, more importantly, would risk making Carrie appear incompetent. In consequence, the other women attempt to help Carrie by slowing their pace just enough to ease the pressure, while still taking pains to maintain just enough speed to avoid arousing suspicions and incriminating themselves.

The first mark up for grabs is earned by coherently explaining the 'predicament' Carrie finds herself in – namely, that she has to keep up an unobtainable pace to avoid creating a backlog. The second mark is for then explaining how the women around Carrie subtly act to alleviate the pressure that has been placed on her.[3]

12. Using the whole passage, explain how the writer uses language to make Carrie's experience attending her first day at work seem intimidating. Use short quotations to support your answer. [8]

The writer successfully creates an air of intimidation as Carrie sets about attending her first day of work through the impersonal and overwhelmingly chaotic portrayal of Fifth Avenue – the road on which her office is based, and down which Carrie walks to get to work. The simile used to describe the road's architecture, likening its makeup to 'a walled canon of brown stone and dark red brick,' lends it an atmosphere of

intimidating authority: a canon is a collection of authoritative books, thus the implication is that the road's architecture resembles to Carrie a set of authoritative texts with which she is woefully unfamiliar. Adding to Fifth Avenue's intimidating air is the chaos that appears to reign: the reader is told how 'men and women, girls and boys were moving onwards in all directions,' the rapid-fire list of people, seemingly moving so quickly that they can only be identified by their sex and age – 'men and women, girls and boys' – enhances the sense of entropy explicitly conjured by the idea of them 'moving... in all directions.'[4]

Interestingly, the writer spells out the intimidating impact this thoroughfare has on Carrie: its tumult explicitly triggers a crisis of confidence in her, as its intimidating unknowability induces in Carrie a sense of insecurity at her own shortfallings: 'Dread at her own inefficiency crept upon her.'

An atmosphere of intimidation is achieved also through the haughty and aloof men Carrie encounters within the workplace: Mr Brown, her first point of contact, is brusque and off-hand ('"What is it you want?" he inquired'), conversationally domineering ('he interrupted'), and impersonal: he refers to her as 'you' and 'the girl,' even though she has just told him her name. The writer again spells out the impact this intimidating manner has on Carrie: we are told at one point, for instance, that 'her heart dropped.' The foreman Carrie encounters next is similarly abrupt and impersonal: he addresses her 'rather sternly,' and his disposition is 'annoyed.' That he refers to another woman in the factory – presumably someone who has worked there some time – merely as 'you' illustrates the pervasiveness of this impersonality.[5]

The writer also infuses Carrie's first day with a sense of menace and intimidation through the labyrinthine architecture of the office itself.[6] Through the course of the text, Carrie is pin-balled through the building: she is shuttled up to the 'fourth floor' in an elevator, travels through storage space and factory space, a transition that sees the ceiling suddenly become lower and more claustrophobic – 'a large, low-ceiled room' – before finally taking another elevator in a 'corner' and winding up on the sixth floor.[7] Insofar as disorientation and intimidation go hand-in-hand, Carrie's disorientating experience in the labyrinthine building is certainly effective in achieving an air of intimidation.

Just as in the previous paper of this kind, the final question takes the form of a mini essay that is asking us to focus on how the author uses language.

Here is the plan I put together before writing the above:

- The overwhelming commute to work.
- Impact of haughty and aloof men in the workplace
- Labyrinthine & disorientating layout of the office building.
- The immediate expectations placed on Carrie to perform.

As you can see, once I started writing, I realised that the plan was likely too long, so I decided to axe my discussion of the immediate pressure to perform Carrie finds herself placed under – even though this discussion would certainly have been relevant, and, if I had pursued it at the expense of one of the themes above, would likely still have won me the marks. When it comes to these mini essays, there are often many ways to skin the cat.

Once again, I am adding a couple of extra paragraphs – one tackling the theme I axed from the essay above, plus one extra theme – in order to demonstrate other ways one might have gone about scoring marks here:

That Carrie – despite her lack of experience – is put to work during the extract's final sequence and placed in the daunting position of being expected to perform efficiently right away, only enhances the overall atmosphere of intimidation.[8] Carrie feels the expectations on her keenly, recognising that she 'had not time to look about,' and finding herself 'bent anxiously to her task:' the expectations are so great that it physically leaves Carrie 'bent' and cowed, while the adverb 'anxiously' spells out the impact of this intimidating circumstance on her emotional state.[9]

Finally, one might note that the air of tentative liberation in the extract's opening sequence in fact heightens the air of intimidation that follows. As Carrie first ventures off to work, she is 'slightly reassured,' and feels as though 'the sunshine of the morning' has dispelled 'fears and misgivings.' By emphasising Carrie's buoyant mood, and the degree to which she has been able to throw off the yoke of negativity, the writer implicitly emphasises the degree to which Fifth Avenue and the office she subsequently encounters are capable of intimidating, for they do not simply intimidate her, but also undo her earlier buoyancy and optimism.

Speculative & Creative Papers

Note: This style of paper is definitely the most idiosyncratic of the bunch; and although a small handful of its questions resemble those we have seen elsewhere, many of its questions are very much distinct. Unlike the other papers, the Speculative and Creative Paper frequently requires the candidate to directly proffer their opinions, make personal judgements, and exercise their powers of imagination.

For those who are more analytically minded, this style of paper can be the most tricky. On the other hand, it also offers many more opportunities for creativity and flair.

Both of the Speculative & Creative papers I've included here are out of a total of forty-one marks.

This extract is taken from a letter sent from the explorer, Robert Walton, to his sister Margaret. The passage recounts events that took place on Walton's ship while attempting to sail to the north pole. It is set during the late eighteenth century.

1   About two o'clock the mist cleared away, and we beheld, stretched out in every direction, vast and irregular plains of ice, which seemed to have no end. Some of my comrades groaned, and my own mind began to grow watchful with anxious thoughts, when a strange sight suddenly attracted our attention and diverted our solicitude

5   from our own situation. We perceived a low carriage, fixed on a sledge and drawn by dogs, pass on towards the north, at the distance of half a mile; a being which had the shape of a man, but apparently of gigantic stature, sat in the sledge and guided the dogs. We watched the rapid progress of the traveller with our telescopes until he was lost among the distant inequalities of the ice.

10 This appearance excited our unqualified wonder. We were, as we believed, many hundred miles from any land; but this apparition seemed to denote that it was not, in reality, so distant as we had supposed. Shut in, however, by ice, it was impossible to follow his track, which we had observed with the greatest attention.

About two hours after this occurrence we heard the ground sea, and before night the

15 ice broke and freed our ship. We, however, lay to until the morning, fearing to encounter in the dark those large loose masses which float about after the breaking up of the ice. I profited of this time to rest for a few hours.

In the morning, however, as soon as it was light, I went upon deck and found all the sailors busy on one side of the vessel, apparently talking to someone in the sea. It was, in fact, a sledge, like that we had seen before, which had drifted towards us in the night on a large fragment of ice. Only one dog remained alive; but there was a human being within it whom the sailors were persuading to enter the vessel. He was not, as the other traveller seemed to be, a savage inhabitant of some undiscovered island, but a European. When I appeared on deck the master said, "Here is our captain, and he will not allow you to perish on the open sea."

On perceiving me, the stranger addressed me in English, although with a foreign accent. "Before I come on board your vessel," said he, "will you have the kindness to inform me whither you are bound?"

You may conceive my astonishment on hearing such a question addressed to me from a man on the brink of destruction and to whom I should have supposed that my vessel would have been a resource which he would not have exchanged for the most precious wealth the earth can afford. I replied, however, that we were on a voyage of discovery towards the northern pole.

Upon hearing this he appeared satisfied and consented to come on board. Good God! Margaret, if you had seen the man who thus capitulated for his safety, your surprise would have been boundless. His limbs were nearly frozen, and his body dreadfully emaciated by fatigue and suffering. I never saw a man in so wretched a condition. We attempted to carry him into the cabin, but as soon as he had quitted the fresh air he fainted. We accordingly brought him back to the deck and restored him to animation by rubbing him with brandy and forcing him to swallow a small quantity. As soon as he showed signs of life we wrapped him up in blankets and placed him near the chimney of the kitchen stove. By slow degrees he recovered and ate a little soup, which restored him wonderfully.

Two days passed in this manner before he was able to speak, and I often feared that his sufferings had deprived him of understanding. When he had in some measure recovered, I removed him to my own cabin and attended on him as much as my duty would permit. I never saw a more interesting creature: his eyes have generally an expression of wildness, and even madness, but there are moments when, if anyone performs an act of kindness towards him or does him any the most trifling service, his whole countenance is lighted up, as it were, with a beam of benevolence and sweetness that I never saw equalled. But he is generally melancholy and despairing, and sometimes he gnashes his teeth, as if impatient of the weight of woes that oppresses him.

When my guest was a little recovered I had great trouble to keep off the men, who wished to ask him a thousand questions; but I would not allow him to be tormented by their idle curiosity, in a state of body and mind whose restoration evidently depended upon entire repose. Once, however, the lieutenant asked why he had come so far upon the ice in so strange a vehicle.

His countenance instantly assumed an aspect of the deepest gloom, and he replied,
60   "To seek one who fled from me."

"And did the man whom you pursued travel in the same fashion?"

"Yes."

"Then I fancy we have seen him, for the day before we picked you up we saw some dogs drawing a sledge, with a man in it, across the ice."

65   This aroused the stranger's attention, and he asked a multitude of questions concerning the route which the dæmon, as he called him, had pursued. Soon after, when he was alone with me, he said, "I have, doubtless, excited your curiosity, as well as that of these good people; but you are too considerate to make inquiries."

"Certainly; it would indeed be very impertinent and inhuman in me to trouble you
70   with any inquisitiveness of mine."

"And yet you rescued me from a strange and perilous situation; you have benevolently restored me to life."

An extract from Mary Shelley's Frankenstein

---

1. The passage describes life on board a ship from over two hundred years ago. Describe THREE ways you think it might differ from life on board a modern-day ship? [3]

2. What do you think Walton means when he writes that his 'mind began to grow watchful with anxious thoughts'?

3. The word 'savage' come from the Latin word 'silvaticus,' which means 'of the woods.' What do you think Walton means when he describes the individual who the stranger was chasing as 'savage'? [4]

4. Re-read the description of the man recovered from lines 44 ('Two days passed...') to 53 ('...that oppresses him'). Choose a phrase from these lines that you think describes the man particularly well and explain why you chose it. [6]

5. The ship's lieutenant asks the stranger why he had come so far across the ice in a sleigh. Outline other lines of questioning you imagine the ship's crew might wish to pursue with the stranger. [8]

6. Re-read the stranger's reaction to the individual he is pursuing (line 59, 'His countenance instantly assumed...', to 68, '...considerate to make inquiries'). What do the writer's choice of words in these lines suggest about the stranger's feelings towards the individual he is pursuing? [4]

7. Look at the portrayal of the stranger's condition in lines 18 ('In the morning...') to 43 ('...restored him wonderfully'). Do you find it surprising that it subsequently takes him two days to recover enough to speak? Give reasons for your answer. [7]

8. Do you think that Robert Walton seems like a good captain? Give reasons for your answer, using details from the passage. [5]

1. The passage describes life on board a ship from over two hundred years ago. Describe THREE ways you think it might differ from life on board a modern-day ship? [3]

a) Whereas it appears that this ship is occupied exclusively by men, one might imagine that a modern-day ship might also have women on board.

b) Whereas the men use outdated means of administering first aid – namely, using brandy to try and revive an individual who has fainted – one might imagine that the occupants of a modern-day ship would focus instead on a victim's blood-flow and breathing.

c) Whereas the occupants of this ship suffer from a lack of visibility, one would imagine that a modern-day ship would have technologies such as radar to solve this issue.

The examiners will not be consulting a list of observations candidates might make. Rather, the examiner is asking you to take a good look at the setting presented, and to identify aspects that we might find odd or out of place. So long as your observations are convincing and sensible, you will secure the marks.

2. What do you think Walton means when he writes that his 'mind began to grow watchful with anxious thoughts'?

That Walton describes his 'mind' as beginning to 'grow watchful' suggests he perceives a difference between merely observing a set of circumstances – which he has already done in the previous sentence – and being 'watchful' with one's mind, which suggests a more intense form of observation that is intertwined with one's thoughts and emotions.[1] The character of Walton's thoughts as he watches is spelt out: they are 'anxious' – though whether the icy terrain is inducing this anxiety, or whether Walton is predisposed to anxiety and is projecting this onto his environs, remains unclear. Yet in any case, the notion that his mind only 'began to grow' this way suggests Walton's anxiety has not yet completely monopolised how he views his environs.[2]

This question is more reminiscent of those we have seen in other papers.

This paper is designating more marks than other papers do for this style of question, but do not be thrown off by this – just remember that any given exam paper you encounter is likely unique to the school you are applying for, and, as a result, the small discrepancy in marks does not necessarily mean you have to answer the question in a wholly different way.

Two marks are likely set aside for demonstrating you understand the content of the quote – that Walton draws a distinction between merely observing something, and being 'watchful' with one's mind; and that the thoughts colouring the process of watching on are ones of anxiety. The other two marks will be for expressing yourself with sophistication and flair.

3. The word 'savage' come from the Latin word 'silvaticus,' which means 'of the woods.' What do you think Walton means when he describes the individual who the stranger was chasing as 'savage'? [4]

Walton, by describing this individual as a 'savage,' is conveying that, judging by appearance, this individual does not appear to have been brought up in what eighteenth century Europeans would have considered civilised society. Rather, his appearance is uncivilised, uncouth, perhaps even regressive and animalistic. That the word stems from the notion of being 'of the woods' augments this air of regression, for the woods might be construed as a symbolic antithesis to civilisation.[3] While the icy plain in which he is spotted is very different to the woods, both places are uncolonised by civilisation: thus the individual's presence in the icy plains is strangely in-keeping with the word's etymology.

If the exam paper is giving you an extra titbit – like, for instance, this information about a word's Latin etymology – the safe thing to do, even if you are not told explicitly to do so, is to work it into your answer.[4]

Above, I am scoring two marks for relaying my understanding of the generally accepted definition of savage as being uncivilised. However, the next two marks are for reflecting on how the etymology of the word offers further insight into the author's use of vocabulary.

4. Re-read the description of the man recovered from lines 44 ('Two days passed...') to 53 ('...that oppresses him'). Choose a phrase from these lines that you think describes the man particularly well and explain why you chose it. [6]

A particularly apt phrase to describe the stranger is that he seems to be 'impatient of the weight of woes.' The idea that he has been labouring under a 'weight of woes' is consistent with his physical and emotional state: he is physically run down to the point that, when first boarding the ship, he falls unconscious, and his reflexive emotional state appears to be one of despondency – and this emotional and physical destitution is what one would expect from such individual.

However, while one might expect someone under a 'weight of woes' to be docile, this stranger appears to still have fight in him, and an urgent desire to throw off the yoke of his woes – hence the aptness of the paradoxical notion that he meets his oppression with impatience.[5] This impatience manifests itself most noticeably in his manic desire to pursue the individual whom we might deduce to be the source of his woes: he even entertains the idea of refusing the ship's help, thus risking certain death, to continue his pursuit. The urgency manifests also in his flashes of 'benevolence' and 'sweetness,' which arguably indicate an impatience to recapture an emotional state that would exist if not for the 'weight' of his oppressive 'woes.'

Of course it is important here to pick out a relevant quote. However, more important than the quote is the explanation of why you think the phrase you have picked is particularly apt.

Notice how I've focused on the paradox at the heart of the phrase I've picked: namely, the fact that the individual is both labouring under a 'weight of woes' – which one would expect might hobble his will to fight – yet is *still* exhibiting extreme impatience. Notice, also, how I underpin my argument with evidence from elsewhere in the extract that demonstrates how the stranger is clearly both labouring under 'weight of woes,' but is also still impatient to liberate himself from these woes.

The quote you pick really should not be more than, say, six words. If you are selective with your choice, this will be more than enough to work with.

5. The ship's lieutenant asks the stranger why he had come so far across the ice in a sleigh. Outline other lines of questioning you imagine the ship's crew might wish to pursue with the stranger. [8]

A preliminary line of questioning the crew might pursue would be to ascertain more about this stranger's identity: they might wish to learn his name – a detail he has not yet surrendered – and to learn more about his background. The crew have heard his European accent; but they might be curious as to where in Europe he hails. However, while the stranger's identity might be a starting point, one would imagine – given the 'gigantic stature' and apparition-like appearance of the individual this stranger was pursuing – that the men would be even more curious to learn about this fleeing individual's identity. Walton notes that the fleeing individual had the appearance of a 'savage inhabitant of some undiscovered island,' so it is probable the crew would want to know where this man came from. They would likely also be curious to understand what accounts for his gigantic size.

Beyond these basics, the most pressing line of questioning would be to try and understand why this stranger is pursuing this 'apparition,' and why is he doing so with such zeal – he has, after all, pursued him all the way into treacherous arctic plains.[6] Also interesting would be to ask whether the stranger had been serious in suggesting that, if the ship not been travelling north, he would have eschewed its help, since it would imply that he considers the pursuit more important than his own life.[7] The fact there was a pursuit in the first place also of course begs the question of what the stranger is intending to do to this individual if he manages to catch him: what is his endgame?

Given the punishing terrain, the crew are likely very curious to learn the route this stranger took to arrive in this location, and whether he had used a combination of different transportation methods to get this far. They would likely be curious, too, about how he had managed to survive up until this point – for instance, how he had managed to source food; how he had been able to fashion himself shelter (if he had managed this at all); and how he had been able to keep himself motivated. They might be curious to know if the stranger has chanced upon any other living

creature while making his journey, and perhaps how the dogs who had been pulling his sleigh had perished.

Finally, the men might be curious to understand more about his conduct aboard thus far. For instance, during his two days of convalescing, they might wonder whether he truly had been wholly unable to respond to their questions as Walton had surmised ('two days passed…before he was able to speak'), or whether he had chosen to stay circumspect for his own reasons.[8] By the same token, they may wonder why he has been so unforthcoming in general since his arrival on board.

This is perhaps the trickiest question in this paper, and the trickiest style of question you will likely encounter during your 11+ comprehension exams as a whole. The question is asking you to speculate; and whereas you might expect it to be worth just a couple of marks, it is in fact the highest scoring question on the paper.

Again, the examiner will not have a mark scheme containing all the "acceptable" answers. After all, this question is explicitly encouraging creativity.

And yet, while this question is encouraging creativity, that does not mean you should be putting in absurd answers. We have some parameters within which to work. We know that the scene is set in the punishing north pole and in the late eighteenth century; we know that the stranger has come at least part of the way in a sleigh, that all but one of his dogs have perished, and that he is pursuing a seemingly gigantic man. We know also that he entertained the idea of rejecting the ship's assistance. Any line of questioning that can be reasonably extrapolated from these parameters will be credited. The possibilities, while perhaps not quite endless, are plentiful.

As ever, before launching into my answer, I put together a quick, bare-bones plan:

- What's his name? What's his country of origin?
- Who is the individual he is pursuing, and what accounts for his enormous size? Why is he pursuing this stranger so obsessively, and for what reason has this individual headed to the arctic? What does he intend to do to this individual?
- Would he really have turned down their help had they not been travelling north?
- How did he manage to get this far by himself, how long did it take him, by which route did he come? How did his dogs wind up dying? How has he been surviving in these punishing arctic conditions?

6. Re-read the stranger's reaction to the individual he is pursuing (line 59, 'His countenance instantly assumed...', to 68, '...considerate to make inquiries'). What do the writer's choice of words in these lines suggest about the stranger's feelings towards the individual he is pursuing? [4]

The writer's choice of words suggests that the stranger feels a great degree of negativity and opprobrium towards the individual he is pursuing.[9] When the stranger first broaches the topic of this individual, his face 'assumes an aspect of the deepest gloom' – his metaphorically darkening face reflecting his dark attitude towards this individual. Moreover, he first refers to the individual as 'one who fled from me,' as if his disdain is too great to give his target a name, and next as a 'daemon,' a word associated with supernatural malignity.[10] Yet while the stranger clearly harbours a profound distaste for this individual, he also seems to exhibit a perverse excitement at the thought of encountering him, as evidenced by the stranger's 'aroused' attention and 'multitude of questions' when he learns the crew had seen his target.

To score four marks, you would want to engage in close analysis of at least two separate words / phrases. Moreover, if the question is asking you to analyse an individual's attitude towards something, and that individual's attitude is divided or nuanced, try to capture that complexity. Notice how, after looking at words and phrases that telegraph the stranger's negativity towards the individual he is pursuing (for instance, 'gloom' and 'daemon'), I invoke evidence to suggest that he also feels some excitement about this individual.

7. Look at the portrayal of the stranger's condition in lines 18 ('In the morning...') to 43 ('...restored him wonderfully'). Do you find it surprising that it subsequently takes him two days to recover enough to speak? Give reasons for your answer. [7]

In many respects it seems unsurprising that the stranger took two days to recover his speech. Walton goes to great lengths to emphasise just how physically incapacitated this stranger was when boarding the ship: Walton observes that 'his limbs were nearly frozen,' and 'his body dreadfully emaciated,' and goes so far as to assert that he 'never saw a man in so wretched condition' – a bold statement from an explorer who one might imagine has faced his fair share of adversity. Walton adds yet more emphasis to the stranger's debilitated state by imagining what his interlocutor, Margaret, would have made of it: 'your surprise would have been boundless.' Moreover, that Walton himself – a first-hand witness – seems unsurprised by the duration of the stranger's convalescence

further encourages the reader to adopt a similar mindset. In fact, during this two-day interim, Walton seems to have feared that the stranger might never recover his mental capacity at all, speculating that 'his suffering' might have 'deprived him of understanding.'[11]

Indeed, even if one was wary that Walton might be employing hyperbole, the fact that the stranger was plucked from this harsh terrain – 'many hundred miles from any land,' and with all but one dog dead – tells the reader that the stranger was still likely to be in a very rundown state. Furthermore, that the stranger fainted almost immediately after boarding the ship seems to largely support Walton's bleak assessment of the stranger's state, thereby again indicating that a two-day recovery period would be unsurprising.

On the other hand, however, one might note that when Walton first encounters the stranger, he speaks articulately and with clarity: 'Before I come on board... whither you are bound?' One might take this as a sign that the stranger is not in such a dire state after all – indeed, his power of speech seems particularly unimpeded – and this arguably invites us to interpret the two-day period of mute recovery as excessive. Furthermore, the very fact that the stranger is asking where Walton's ship is 'bound' – a question that, as Walton observes, implies that the man is willing to decline their aid should they be heading in a different direction – further suggests that the stranger's condition could still have been far worse. Finally, one might note that the stranger receives outstanding care from the crew, as illustrated by the way they place him by 'the kitchen stove' and 'feed him soup,' which again might invite the reader to feel some surprise that the stranger takes some two days to recover his speech.

On the whole, I am unsurprised by the two-day recovery period; after all, even if one decides to take Walton's description of the stranger's state with a pinch of salt, the punishing environs in which the stranger has been operating and the fact he faints suggests he was in a extremely precarious state which would have required a hefty recovery period.

The 'Do you find X surprising?' is another classic question in the Creative and Speculative Paper. The secret here is to explore both sides of the argument in depth (and with quotations!), and then (and this is important) come to a verdict. It usually does not matter which side you pick in the end. The important thing is that you can justify your choice.

You will notice that often when answering comprehension questions I try and avoid using the word 'I,' because I generally think it is more scholarly to avoid it, and to say things like: 'one may argue' or 'one might observe.' However, this sort of question is explicitly asking us to give our opinion, so using 'I' is essential (indeed, the Creative and Speculative Paper is, as a whole, far more personal than the others, and encourages this personalised response).

Here is the plan I quickly threw together before I started writing:

- Unsurprising: The sheer extent of the stranger's injuries, the fact that he faints, and the fact that his dogs have all perished. The sheer harshness of the territory. Moreover, Walton himself is unsurprised.
- Surprising: The fact that he contemplated turning down the help might suggest he was more hardy. Although he falls into silence, he is talking just fine beforehand. He is receiving fantastic care from the men.
- Overall: not surprising, due to harsh terrain.

8. Do you think that Robert Walton seems like a good captain? Give reasons for your answer, using details from the passage. [5]

Insofar as one might deem a "good" captain to be someone who is capable of displaying compassion towards those he oversees, Walton certainly seems to fit the bill. Walton's compassion and empathy are on show throughout the extract: not only does he ensure that the stranger receives the best care when he boards the ship, but he goes above and beyond: he lodges the stranger in his 'own cabin' and 'attended on him' personally. Moreover, that this act of compassion is not a one-off is evidenced by the fact that his crew expect him to act with kindness – the crew, for instance, tell the stranger that their captain 'will not allow [him] to perish on the open sea' – thereby indicating that Walton likely has a track-record of such behaviour. Walton's decision to have his ship 'lay to until morning,' due to concerns about 'loose masses' of ice, also demonstrate a pragmatic restraint and prudence that one would expect from a wise captain: unwilling to take foolish risks, he errs on the side of caution.[12]

However, while Walton demonstrates admirable caution with regards to the rogue icebergs, at other times he demonstrates a disturbing lack of caution. A key example would be his *laissez-faire* approach towards the stranger's identity.[13] Although the stranger was found under highly unusual circumstances, and, even before he conceded as much, was clearly linked in some way to the man of 'gigantic statue,' Walton does not deem it prudent to ascertain whether this individual could in some

way endanger his ship – that is, whether he might be dangerous in his own right, or perhaps dangerous insofar as he might attract hostile forces. Instead, Walton shies away from quizzing him for days on end (he fears being 'impertinent and inhuman' with his 'inquisitiveness') and does not even discover his name. One might also note that there is a strange naivety to Walton: he seems to construe the stranger as a kind of transcendent being – he talks of the stranger exhibiting 'benevolence and sweetness that [he] never saw equalled' – and this seems to further cloud his decision-making.[14] Finally, one might accuse Walton of lacking leadership: early on in the extract, when the men 'groaned' at the sight of seemingly endless ice, Walton does not rally their spirit, but instead allows the negativity to infect him, too: he 'grew watchful with anxious thoughts.'

On the whole, while Walton exhibits a admirable capacity for empathy, he falls short of the title of a "good" captain, for in fact his empathy at times seems to compromise his ability to make sound decisions, such as attempting to ascertain the stranger's identity.

This question is fairly similar to the one beforehand, yet is asking us to judge a character rather than a situation / a character's opinion.

Again, it is important to discuss both sides of the argument while drawing on quotations from the passage, and then to make a well-reasoned personal verdict. However, since this question is worth fewer marks than the one beforehand, you will want to make it slightly shorter and sharper.

Here is the brief plan I put together prior to writing:

- Good captain: Empathetic: both in his actions, but also seemingly on a historical basis, since the crew expect him to behave empathetically. Admirably cautious in a way that safeguards his crew: he wishes to avoid colliding with ice at night.
- Bad captain: Not cautious enough in other ways: he makes no efforts to vet the stranger, despite the fact he might be dangerous. Gives the stranger nearly endless latitude – potentially too empathetic? There is also a naivety to him – potentially lacks leadership skills?
- Overall a bad captain, due to naive decision making.

This extract is taken from a novel set in Europe during the early 1900s, and recounts Philip's experiences as he arrives back at an apartment he shares with Mildred, a woman with whom he is in a relationship.

1   Philip would have liked to drive on further, it was distasteful to him to go back to his
rooms, and he wanted the air; but the desire to see the child clutched suddenly at his
heartstrings, and he smiled to himself as he thought of her toddling towards him with
a crow of delight. He was surprised, when he reached the house and looked up

5   mechanically at the windows, to see that there was no light. He went upstairs and
knocked, but got no answer. When Mildred went out she left the key under the mat
and he found it there now. He let himself in and going into the sitting-room struck a
match. Something had happened, he did not at once know what; he turned the gas
on full and lit it; the room was suddenly filled with the glare and he looked round. He

10   gasped.

The whole place was wrecked. Everything in it had been wilfully destroyed. Anger
seized him, and he rushed into Mildred's room. It was dark and empty. When he had
got a light he saw that she had taken away all her things and the baby's (he had
noticed on entering that the go-cart was not in its usual place on the landing, but

15   thought Mildred had taken the baby out;) and all the things on the washing-stand had
been broken, a knife had been drawn cross-ways through the seats of the two chairs,
the pillow had been slit open, there were large gashes in the sheets and the counter-
pane, the looking-glass appeared to have been broken with a hammer. Philip was

bewildered. He went into his own room, and here too everything was in confusion.
20 The basin and the ewer had been smashed, the looking-glass was in fragments, and
the sheets were in ribands. Mildred had made a slit large enough to put her hand into
the pillow and had scattered the feathers about the room. She had jabbed a knife into
the blankets. On the dressing-table were photographs of Philip's mother, the frames
had been smashed and the glass shivered. Philip went into the tiny kitchen. Every-
25 thing that was breakable was broken, glasses, pudding-basins, plates, dishes.

It took Philip's breath away. Mildred had left no letter, nothing but this ruin to mark
her anger, and he could imagine the set face with which she had gone about her
work. He went back into the sitting-room and looked about him. He was so aston-
ished that he no longer felt angry. He looked curiously at the kitchen-knife and the
30 coal-hammer, which were lying on the table where she had left them. Then his eye
caught a large carving-knife in the fireplace which had been broken. It must have
taken her a long time to do so much damage. Lawson's portrait of him had been cut
cross-ways and gaped hideously. His own drawings had been ripped in pieces; and the
photographs, Manet's Olympia and the Odalisque of Ingres, the portrait of Philip
35 IV, had been smashed with great blows of the coal-hammer. There were gashes in the
table-cloth and in the curtains and in the two arm-chairs. They were quite ruined.
On one wall over the table which Philip used as his desk was the little bit of Persian
rug which Cronshaw had given him. Mildred had always hated it.

"If it's a rug it ought to go on the floor," she said, "and it's a dirty stinking bit of stuff,
40 that's all it is."

It made her furious because Philip told her it contained the answer to a great riddle.
She thought he was making fun of her. She had drawn the knife right through it three
times, it must have required some strength, and it hung now in tatters. Philip had two
or three blue and white plates, of no value, but he had bought them one by one for
45 very small sums and liked them for their associations. They littered the floor in fragments. There were long gashes on the backs of his books, and she had taken the
trouble to tear pages out of the unbound French ones. The little ornaments on the
chimney-piece lay on the hearth in bits. Everything that it had been possible to
destroy with a knife or a hammer was destroyed.

50 The whole of Philip's belongings would not have sold for thirty pounds, but most of
them were old friends, and he was a domestic creature, attached to all those odds and
ends because they were his; he had been proud of his little home, and on so little
money had made it pretty and characteristic. He sank down now in despair. He asked
himself how she could have been so cruel. A sudden fear got him on his feet again
55 and into the passage, where stood a cupboard in which he kept his clothes. He
opened it and gave a sigh of relief. She had apparently forgotten it and none of his
things was touched.

He went back into the sitting-room and, surveying the scene, wondered what to do; he had not the heart to begin trying to set things straight; besides there was no food in
60 the house, and he was hungry. He went out and got himself something to eat. When he came in he was cooler. A little pang seized him as he thought of the child, and he wondered whether she would miss him, at first perhaps, but in a week she would have forgotten him; and he was thankful to be rid of Mildred. He did not think of her with wrath, but with an overwhelming sense of boredom.

65 "I hope to God I never see her again," he said aloud.

An extract from Somerset Maugham's Of Human Bondage

1. The passage describes an apartment from almost a hundred year ago. Describe THREE ways you think it might differ from a modern-day apartment? [3]

2. What do you think the writer means when he refers to Philip's desire to see his child as 'clutching at his heartstrings.' (lines 2-3)? [4]

3. The word 'mechanically' comes from the word 'mechanic,' which in Middle English meant 'relating to manual labour.' What do you think the writer means when he describes Philip as looking up at the windows 'mechanically'? [4]

4. Re-read the sequence that narrates the first moments after Philip sets eyes on his apartment. (lines 11, 'The whole place was…', to 25… 'plates, dishes'). Choose two phrases from these lines that you think describes the state of affairs in the apartment particularly well and explain why you chose it. [6]

5. At lines 46-47, the reader is told that 'there were long gashes on the backs of his books, and [Mildred] had taken the trouble to tear pages out of the unbound French ones.' Discuss the types of books you think Philip might have in his possession. [8]

6. Re-read the section about the Persian rug (37, 'On one wall over…' to 43, '…hung now in tatters'). What do the writer's choice of words in these lines suggest about Mildred's feelings towards the rug? [4]

7. Do you think that Philip is right to regard Mildred as 'so cruel'? Give reasons for your answer, mentioning things in the passage that have led you to this conclusion. [7]

8. Do you think Philip is an individual in control of his emotions? Give reasons for your answer, using details from the passage. [5]

1. The passage describes an apartment from almost a hundred year ago. Describe THREE ways you think it might differ from a modern-day apartment? [3]

- **Whereas the lights in Mildred and Philip's apartment appear to be powered by gas, one would expect a modern apartment to have electrical lights.**
- **Whereas Philip has a basin in his bedroom, in most modern day apartments one would not expect to find the basin in the bathroom instead.**
- **Whereas there is no mention of technology in this apartment, one would expect a modern-day apartment to contain such things as radios, televisions or computers.**

Again, the trick here is to go a step beyond merely picking up on details – you also need to intelligently weigh what you see here against your own expectations and experiences. You will be credited for any sensible point.

2. What do you think the writer means when he refers to Philip's desire to see his child as 'clutching at his heartstrings.' (lines 2-3)? [4]

> **By referring to Philip's desire as 'clutching at his heartstrings,' the writer is making use of the heart's symbolic association with strong emotions – particularly those of love and sorrow – to suggest that Philip's**

desire to see his son functions to induce these emotions in him. The metaphor of 'clutching at... heartstrings' invites the reader to envisage Philip's heartstrings as something that might be physically strummed (indeed, 'clutching' is an even more wrenching verb) in a way that would elicit a powerful emotive response, and to envisage his abstract desire to see his son as 'clutching at his heartstring' in just such a fashion.

Two marks here are for acknowledging that the author is making use of the heart's symbolic status as the organ responsible for powerful emotions, and understanding that the author is suggesting that thoughts of the child induces strong emotions in Philip. Two further marks are for coherently and maturely delving into the minutiae of the metaphor (the examiner will want to see the word metaphor in your answer!), and the image it conjures of Philip's heartstrings being physically manhandled.

3. The word 'mechanically' comes from the word 'mechanic,' which in Middle English meant 'relating to manual labour.' What do you think the writer means when he describes Philip as looking up at the windows 'mechanically'? [4]

The writer, by stating that Philip looks at the windows 'mechanically,' is suggesting that Philip's motion is comparable to that of a machine: it implies not only that the gesture is unthinking (and thus perhaps one he undertakes routinely), but also that the actual motion of his head resembles the motion one might expect from a robot. Moreover, insofar as mechanisms and machines are tools to carry out work, one might infer that the writer is suggesting that Philip's gesture as he checks in with Mildred is a kind of labour – an interpretation augmented by the fact that 'mechanic' in Middle English had connotations of manual labour.

To secure the first two marks, you need to demonstrate that you understand the most obvious meanings of the word mechanically, and what they imply about Philip's body language (that he moves unthinkingly, jerkily, in a way reminiscent of a machine). The next two marks are for discussing the idea specifically of 'mechanically' also having connotations of physical labour – i.e. for Philip, looking at the window is a kind of work – and how the word's roots emphasise this interpretation.

4. Re-read the sequence that narrates the first moments after Philip sets eyes on his apartment. (lines 11, 'The whole place was...', to 25 '...plates, dishes'). Choose two

phrases from these lines that you think describes the state of affairs in the apartment particularly well and explain why you chose it. [6]

A particularly apt phrase the writer uses to convey the state of the apartment is the observation, as Philip enters his bedroom, that 'here too everything was in confusion.' The idea of 'confusion' not only suggests that the items within the bedroom are in a state of chaotic disarray, but it also functions to personify the entire contents of the room, suggesting that every last item ('everything') been plunged into a state of psychological 'confusion' after the assault the room had undergone. Moreover, the phrase subtly hints that the chaos also induces confusion, since Philip himself is arguably encompassed by the word 'everything.'

Another phrase that is particular effective in conveying the state of affairs in the apartment is the observation that 'Everything that was breakable was broken.' While the word 'everything,' which appeared in the previous quote, once again implies ubiquity, the idea that everything 'breakable was broken' draws attention to the fastidiousness and precision that went into the destruction.[1] Moreover, identifying item as 'breakable' serves to deprive them of any other function or meaning beyond their capacity to be broken, lending an air of fatalism to the circumstance within the apartment.[2]

Whereas in the equivalent question in the previous paper we were asked to pick out just one phrase to analyse, this time we have been asked to extract two; yet, like last time, there are still six marks in play. This tells us that our analysis of each of the two phrases can be somewhat less meaty: they are each worth three marks, as opposed to six.

Again, notice that the two phrases I've picked out are both six words: I'm keeping them short and sweet. You will notice also that in each paragraph I have used the word 'moreover,' which is a sign that I have made at least two quick arguments. This is to pre-empt any accusations that my analysis is too brief: I don't want to give the examiner an excuse to cap either of these paragraphs at two marks

5. At lines 46-47 the reader is told that 'there were long gashes on the backs of his books, and [Mildred] had taken the trouble to tear pages out of the unbound French ones.' Discuss the types of books you think Philip might have in his possession. [8]

Given Philip's affection for the Persian rug he received from Cronshaw, one might expect that his interest in the Middle East to be reflected in his personal library: perhaps he might have books on the history of the region, or perhaps atlases or travel books on the area. Philips also had a photo reproduction of 'Odalisque of Ingres,' which refers to a French painting from the Romantic period. As a result, one might speculate that Philips possibly had books on other Romantic era artists – perhaps biographies of these artists; perhaps books containing further photographs – but also may have an interest in Romantic era writers, too: for instance, he may have poetry collections from the likes of William Wordsworth or John Keats, for example.

Since the text makes explicit reference to 'unbound French books,' it would be reasonable to speculate that Philips have both fiction and non-fiction volumes written in French: perhaps he has a book of poetry from a seminal French poet such as Baudelaire, and a philosophical tract from a seminal French thinker such as Rousseau. Moreover, given Philip's evident Francophilia and his interest in Romantic-era art, one would almost certainly to find books pertaining to the late eighteenth century's French Revolution – the seminal historic event that shaped so much of the Romantic era in Europe.[3]

Philip also has a clear interest in portraiture (he has a portrait of both of himself by an individual called 'Lawson', as well as a one of King Philip IV), so one might expect to find books relating to portraiture in general – be they instructional guides on how to paint a portrait, or art history books on portraiture. The portrait of King Philip IV – a Spanish monarch – may also hint at a wider interest in Spanish history, Spanish art (the portrait was originally done by a Spanish artist), as well as monarchical histories in general. As a result, one might expect to find books relating to any one of these topics within Philip's personal library.

There may also be more practical books in Philip's collection: for example, an instruction manual on how to effectively operate a coal fireplace – a feature within his apartment – or even a book on childcare, since the passage makes clear there is a child in his life. One might also not be too surprised to find a compendium of riddles: Philip likened his rug to a riddle, which might hint that he is an individual who enjoys riddles enough to have an anthology of them.

This is another of these fiendish speculative questions: it seems innocuous enough, but then you realise there are eight marks in play.

Again, lean into the creativity this style of question invites. We know that the novel is set in Europe in the early 1900s, and that Philip has an affection for his Persian rug, as well as European artists (many of whom are named specifically) and portraiture more broadly. We know also that he has some French books, and a portrait of a King Philip IV of Spain. We have also been informed of other aspects of his life – the fact there is a child in his life; the sort of furniture in his apartment. So long as the ideas you proffer do not clash terribly with these details, you have free rein.

6. Re-read the section about the Persian rug (37, 'One one wall...', to 43, '...hung now in tatters.'). What do the writer's choice of words in these lines suggest about Mildred's feelings towards the rug? [4]

Although the observation that 'Mildred had always hated' the rug gives a clear indication of Mildred's antipathy towards the rug, there is more nuance. The reader learns that the rug made her 'furious' as a result of Philip telling her it 'contained the answer to a great riddle,' which made her feel as if she was the butt of a joke ('thought... he was making fun of her'). From this, one can infer that Mildred saw the rug as a symbol of what she perceived to be Philip's sense of superiority over her: a 'riddle' she could not divine, but he could. Consequently, the writer's choice of words here indicate that Mildred's feelings towards the rug are intimately linked to her feelings towards Philip, and thus her comment that 'it's a dirty stinking bit of stuff' – a comment that suggests the rug is physically disgusting – functions to spell out her antagonism towards Philip, too.

The top-line takeaway – which will win the candidate two marks if explained coherently, with judiciously chosen quotes – is that Mildred hated the rug. However, to score a further two marks, the student needs to grapple with Mildred's reaction to Philip's characterisation of the rug's pattern as a 'riddle,' and how she construes the rug as a symbol of (what she perceives to be) Philip's disdain for her.

Yes, those extra two marks are tough to come by. But this wouldn't be a devilishly hard paper if they weren't!

7. Do you think that Philip is right to regard Mildred as 'so cruel'? Give reasons for your answer, mentioning things in the passage that have led you to this conclusion. [7]

A key issue in deciding whether to characterise Mildred as 'cruel' is the difficulty in establishing whether Mildred was definitely responsible for the damage to the apartment – this is something Philip assumes, yet something for which he has no definitive proof. That said, if Mildred *was* responsible, she might be considered 'cruel' in many respects. It is clear that Philip is greatly invested in the child who appeared to cohabit with the couple: thinking of the child 'clutches at his heartstrings' and induces 'a little pang.' As a result, by taking the child without warning and leaving Philip unsure whether he will see the child again, Mildred had surely acted cruelly. Furthermore, if Mildred had indeed been the one to destroy Philip's possessions, she had cruelly made sure to target those items that were most dear to Philip: for instance, the 'blue and white plates' Philip had liked not for their price, but 'for their associations,' and the 'Persian rug' that Philip had liked enough to hang.

Yet the cruellest instances of destruction are arguably those targeting the portrait of Philip and the 'photographs of Philip's mother,' for these not-so-subtly hint at a desire to enact bodily violence against both Philip personally and his nearest and dearest.

However, there is also good reason to dispute the characterisation of Mildred as 'so cruel.' Aside from the fact that Mildred may not have even been responsible for the damage, there is also a lack of context: even if Mildred had been responsible, Philip may have provoked her in a way commensurate with the damage done.[4] Indeed, Philip's comments that the rug resembled a 'riddle,' which Mildred had construed as a joke at her expense, might hint that Philip had a history of antagonising her. However, even if Mildred had enacted this damage with no provocation, there may still be grounds to dispute the idea that Mildred is 'so cruel.' The fact, for instance, that 'everything...breakable was broken' indicates that Mildred might have acted not with vindictive premeditation, but indiscriminately, thereby potentially undercutting the superlative that she was 'so' cruel. One might also note that the 'cupboard in which [Philip] kept his clothes' had not been targeted, which might indicate that Mildred displayed a degree of mercy – Philip believes the cupboard was something she had merely 'forgotten' about, but again this is not something that can be proved.

On the whole, assuming that Mildred was indeed responsible for the damage and that Philip had not provoked her in any substantive way, I believe it is fair to characterise Mildred as 'so cruel.' After all, not only does taking the child represent a huge emotional blow, but Philip was

also deeply attached to his belongings, going so far as to call them 'old friends.'

––––––––

Although this question is slightly different to the seven mark, 'do you find it surprising' style question we saw in the previous paper, it is very similar in how it functions. This time, however, we are being asked to make a judgement on a character's opinion.

Due to the deep similarities between this question and the seven-marker in the previous paper, I have adopted an almost identical approach. First, I have a paragraph (full of evidence from the text) covering the reasons to support Philip's characterisation of Mildred; next, I have a paragraph outlining reasons that might make Philip's characterisation appear more shaky. Finally, I offer my personal verdict.

Look at it this way: your 'for' and 'against' paragraphs are both worth three marks apiece. And to avoid losing marks, you need to ensure that both of these paragraphs contain at least a couple of convincing reasons, as well as relevant quotes from the text. The final mark is for offering a well-reasoned final verdict; and make sure to use the word 'I' – after all, they are asking for your personal opinion.

Here's a short plan I put together before I started writing.

- Cruel: Taking away the child, especially without warning. The attack on the portrait is particularly antagonistic: the threat of bodily violence. The focus on minutiae shows a vindictiveness.
- Not so cruel: Are we sure she did it? If she did, does context not matter – perhaps Philip had provoked her in some way? Her indiscriminate approach might indicate less cruelty, since it hints at a lack of premeditation. She also spared his clothes (though was this on purpose?)
- Ultimately, if Mildred was responsible, she ought to be considered cruel, for Philip was deeply attached to his possessions.

As an aside, you will also notice that in my answer I raise the prospect that perhaps Mildred was not responsible for the damage at all, since we have no proof beyond Philip's assumption. The examiner will likely not expect this line of argument; but if you can make a convincing point of this kind – that is, a point that reads between the lines, and can be cogently argued – it will impress. However, before you make such an argument, be sure it can be sustained by the text!

8. Do you think Philip is an individual in control of his emotions? Give reasons for your answer, using details from the passage. [5]

Perhaps the most compelling indication that Philip has a handle on his emotions is the fact that he proves capable of moving through his apartment and registering minutiae, which implicitly telegraphs composure. The matter-of-fact, unceremonious way in which Philip's movements are narrated – 'went into his own room;' 'went into the tiny kitchen' – cements the sense of deliberateness to his examination, whereas his sober presence of mind is communicated through a litany of detailed lists: 'glasses, pudding-basins, plates, dishes.' However, there are even more explicit indications that Philip has a handle on his emotions. Near the end of the extract, Philip is able to detach himself from the trauma of the scene enough to leave and get a meal – 'he went out and got... something to eat' – which not only indicates self-control, but also functions as a mechanism to soothe his emotions: the reader is told he returned 'cooler.' Moreover, while there are many indications that Mildred has pushed his emotional buttons – for instance, by taking the child – he does not fall victim to anger, an emotion associated with a loss of control. Rather, instead of 'wrath,' he thinks of Mildred with 'boredom.'

Yet while Philip may seem calm enough to give the apartment a thorough once-over, the writer does use lexicon to suggest that Philip's emotions have been pushed to their limits: he 'gasped' on first setting eyes on the apartment, and the tableau as a whole is said to have taken 'Philip's breath away' – two physical response associated with an overwhelming sense of shock. Interestingly, when Philip's thoughts turn to his clothes cupboard, the narrator observes that 'a sudden fear got him on his feet again,' the phraseology suggesting that the fear overrode Philip's free will and 'got him on his feet.' Finally, one might argue that the fact Philip slips into the assumption that Mildred was behind this potentially suggests that his emotions have shut off his ability to entertain other possibilities.

Although there are flashes of intense emotion that take their toll on Philip in the moment, he largely proves capable of taming and controlling his emotions, and keeping at bay those emotions – particularly anger – that would be most likely to render him 'out of control.'

This answer takes a similar format to the last, though this time we are being asked to make a judgment on the protagonist. Two marks will be rewarded for a well reasoned argument (augmented with quotes) to justify characterising Philip as 'in control' of his emotions, and two for a strong argument against the proposition. Again, the final mark is reserved for your verdict, which must be backed by a convincing line of reasoning.

As ever, here is the plan I put together beforehand:

- In control: He has the composure to walk around and take in minutiae. His measured response to not seeing his child. The handle he has on his anger: hunger seems to take priority.
- Not in control: Lexicon implies that his emotions are at an extreme. Makes emotive assumptions and judgments.
- More in control than not, despite flashes of extreme emotion.

Endnotes

Paper One: Model Answers & Guidance

1. The word aesthetic basically refers to how things look.
2. If something is in a state of flux, it means that it is constantly changing.
3. Onomatopoeia is when a word sounds like the thing it refers to. Examples include bang, crash and pop.
4. If you are extricating yourself from somewhere, it means you are removing yourself from that location.
5. Staccato is a word that is chiefly used in music. However, when used to describe language, it implies the words or phrase are short and jarring.

    Put simply, if you are experiencing something vicariously, it means you are experiencing it through someone else. It's a really great word for comprehensions.

    Cadaver is another word for a dead body!
6. If something is tacit, it means that it is not said explicitly, but it is still something we can infer.
7. If you are paranoid, it means that you believe that people are out to get you!
8. You can usually spot a interpolated phrase by watching out for a snippet of text that is enclosed on either side by a comma or a dash; and you can tell it is an interpolated phrase because, if you remove it altogether, the sentence will still make sense without it. What I'm arguing here is that the interpolated phrase itself looks almost as if it is being strangled by the dashes on either side of it.

    Asphyxiation is another word for suffocation.
9. A cataclysm is a huge disastrous event.
10. To be fastidious is to be excessively diligent and thorough.
11. To galvanise someone is to trigger them into doing something.
12. To dissemble is to put on an act and deceive.
13. To be hubristic is a bit like being confident to the point of arrogance.
14. The minutiae basically refers to the smallest details.
15. To parse something is to break it down into its constituent elements.
16. Stimuli refers to anything that stimulates the senses (sight, touch, hearing, taste, smell)
17. If someone has no compunction it means they have no remorse.

Paper Two: Model Answers & Guidance

1. Offering a quick definition of the word Gothic is tricky. In short, it is the sort of stuff you expect from "horror" stories: haunted houses, supernatural forces, creepy twins, monsters – in short, things that generally make you feel uneasy.
2. If something is idiosyncratic, it means it is unusual.
3. A Gothic outsider is a bit like a monster: someone who is not like everyone else, who does not seem to belong. Monsters are not always bad. They are sometimes merely misunderstood.
4. If someone has a sense of foreboding, it means they have a sense that something bad is set to happen.
5. If someone is aloof, it means they are emotionally distant and unavailable.
6. When I say that the writer dissects the city into 'disparate...parts,' I mean that he is kind of breaking it down into its different elements.

    To allay something is to make it go away, or to make it less extreme/impactful.
7. When I say that the verb 'worrying' is given 'physical literalism' I'm observing the fact that the author has basically used it instead of a verb like 'clutching' or 'rubbing,' which implies that 'worrying' is something you can do physically, instead of it just taking place inside the brain.
8. If someone is brusque, it means they are abrupt and short with their speech.
9. A monosyllabic word is one with just one syllable.
10. If someone is meticulous, it means they are excessively thorough and exact.

11. A voyeur is someone who watches others. Although the word often has sexual undertones, it can be used in less sexual contexts.
12. If someone has a proclivity for watching others, it means that they have a tendency for doing so.
13. To be nihilistic is to have a bleak, fatalistic view of the world and existence.

Paper Three: Model Answers & Guidance

1. If one thing is akin to another, it means they are similar.
2. If two people are cohabiting, it means they are living together in the same place.
3. If you feel antipathy towards someone, it means you feel something akin to hatred towards them.
4. To be coddled is to be treated in an overprotective way.
5. To take umbrage is to take offence.
6. To save face means to avoid embarrassment or humiliation.
7. Obliquely means indirectly. So to bring something up obliquely means to bring it up in a roundabout way.
8. A cryptic comment is one that is difficult to decipher.
9. If I make a comment, and it goes over your head, it means that you have failed to understand what I mean.
10. If someone is pragmatic, it means they are practical and willing to adapt to circumstances.
11. The word reciprocate means something akin to paying back in kind. If someone told me they loved me, and I told them I reciprocate, it means I love them too.
12. If something (an event, a comment) is acrimonious, it means that it is characterised by conflict and ill-will.
13. The provenance of something – be it a quote, or a photo – is where that thing originates from. By saying that we do not know the specific provenance of this quote, I am observing that we do not know who, exactly, said it: it might have been any one of Gilly's friends.
14. If someone behaves cravenly, it means they are behaving in a cowardly way.
15. Pacifism is a philosophical stance that opposes war.
16. A paradox is when you have two contradictory ideas in tandem (indeed, an oxymoron is a type of paradox – a linguistic one). Another example of a paradox is the idea that God might make a stone so heavy that even he could not move it. The immovability of the stone clashes with the idea of God as an infinitely powerful being.
17. An altercation is another word for an argument.
18. To be ostracised is to be excluded.
    If someone is naive, it means that they have an overly innocent view of the world.
19. If someone is behaving histrionically, it means they are behaving overdramatically – or even melo-dramatically.

Paper Four: Model Answers & Guidance

1. An oxymoron is a phrase that combines two contradictory ideas. A famous one is spoken by Shakespeare's Romeo: 'O loving hate!' The ideas of love and hate are contradictory, hence this is an oxymoron.
    To have gravitas is to have an air of authority.
2. If something is enigmatic, it is ambiguous and elusive.
3. A euphemism is when something is expressed indirectly. They are often used when someone is trying to convey something rude or unsavoury, but does not wish to put things in stark terms.
4. To sate one's appetite is to satisfy it.
5. To be irreverent is to be disrespectful to authority, or the way things are usually done.
6. The word profane means something similar to blasphemous.
7. A vignette is a short sequence. In a sense, pretty much all of these extracts could be called vignettes.
8. The idiom 'to hold court' basically means to take the lead in a conversation.
9. The word interlocutor is used to describe someone being spoken to. As you read this, you are my interlocutor!
    If something is ancillary, it means it is secondary to a primary, more important function.
10. Multitudinous basically means many.

11. If someone is speaking hyperbolically, it means they are using lots of exaggeration.
12. If something is outlandish, it is bizarre and unusual.
13. Verbatim means word for word. I'm basically pointing out that whereas we are told exactly what the other characters say, the narrator merely paraphrases Ridley's speech.

Paper Five: Model Answers & Guidance

1. To usurp is to take over. If someone violently took over the government, for instance, we might say they have usurped power.
   Here, we are talking about Jo's agency — that is, her ability to exert her own free will. I am arguing that this personified anger has "taken over" Jo's ability to exercise free will.
2. A writer's lexicon is their choice of words.
   To transgress is to do something wrong. A transgression is sort of like a sin.
   A deity is a kind of god.
3. Kinesis refers to movement.
4. Chekov was a Russian playwright, and he famously noted that if a gun appears in a work of fiction, it needs to go off at some point before the end of the story. He was trying to get across the idea that there should be no unnecessary details: if something is mentioned, the writer should make use of it at some point. So I'm basically arguing that the fact the threat of thin ice has been mentioned ought to be a warning to the reader that it is not just an incidental detail, but something that will later turn out to be pivotal to the plot.
5. The word frenetic means something along the lines of wild and out of control.
6. Juxtaposition is when you contrast two very different things, and, through this comparison, draw attention to their differences.

Paper Six: Model Answers & Guidance

1. Temporality refers to the quality of being temporary.
   To be ascendant means to be in the position of power. I'm saying that once the sun goes back in again, the fears will re-emerge.
2. To compound something is to make it worse!
3. If you are alleviating the pressure on someone, you are reducing the pressure on them.
4. Entropy means something similar to chaos.
5. An impersonal work environment would be an environment where there is very little meaningful inter-human interaction.
6. A labyrinth is like a really complex maze. If something is labyrinthine, it is thus deeply mazelike.
7. Claustrophobia is a fear of small spaces. If a place is described as claustrophobic, it means it is a space that induces a sense of claustrophobia in those within in.
8. If a situation is daunting, it means its intimidating and overwhelming.
9. To be cowed is to be forced to submit.

Paper Seven: Model Answers & Guidance

1. Another word for intertwined would be interwoven. I'm saying that Walton's thoughts and emotions here are tangled together.
2. I'm using the word monopolise here as a synonym for dominate. I'm arguing that while Walton is becoming more anxious, the anxiety is not completely dominating his mind.
3. Augments means enhances or emphasises.
   Antithesis is a synonym for opposite.
4. The etymology of a word is where that word comes from. For instance, a lot of words in English have Latin etymology, which means that they are adapted from words from the Latin language.
5. To be docile is to be weak and compliant.
6. To be zealous is to be extremely passionate.
7. To eschew somebody's help is to reject their help.
8. To convalesce is to recover from an illness.

9. If you level opprobrium at someone, you are criticising them in harsh terms.
10. To be malign is to be evil or poisonous.
11. An interim is a space of time between two events.
12. If someone is prudent, it means they make sensible decisions.
13. Laissez-faire is a French term which has entered into English parlance. It means 'to leave alone.' I'm trying to communicate the fact that Walton takes little to no action to unearth the stranger's identity and personal history.
14. If someone is transcendent, it means they are divine or even godly. I'm arguing that, at least to some extent, this is how Walton seems to perceive this stranger.

Paper Eight: Model Answers & Guidance

1. Ubiquity means something akin to 'all-encompassing' or 'everywhere.' Religious people tend to think of God as ubiquitous, for example.
2. To be fatalistic is to believe that everything is governed by fate, and thus there is no reason to be anything but resigned. I am arguing that the author's turn of phrase here almost suggests that it was inevitable that these items were going to end up broken.
3. A Francophile is someone who loves France and its culture.
4. Commensurate means in proportion to.